# VEG – simple, stylish and seasonal vegetarian cooking

# VEG – simple, stylish and seasonal vegetarian cooking

Catherine Mason

Pauntley
Press

Published by Pauntley Press
An imprint of Ford & Mason Ltd
Compton House, Redmarley, Gloucestershire, GL19 3JB, UK

www.pauntley-press.co.uk

British Library Cataloguing-in-Publication Data
A catalogue record for this book is available from The British Library

ISBN: 0 9534897 2 8

Printed and bound in Great Britain by Cedar Press, Bristol
Cover by creativenatives, Bristol

10  9  8  7  6  5  4  3  2  1

# CONTENTS

# MAIN COURSES 61

# FREEZER AND PANTRY

# INDEX

# ACKNOWLEDGEMENTS

The following people have helped in numerous ways, directly and indirectly, with the long process of bringing this book to completion.

Euan Greig, Chris Kennedy, Ann Kingaby, Oliver Lee, Ruth Moulton, Adaire Osbaldestone, Bernadette Stokoe and Fran Winston all read the manuscript painstakingly, picked up numerous problems and inconsistencies and made all manner of helpful suggestions. Special thanks to Liz Oppedijk, whose contribution in this area was positively heroic. The book is undoubtedly better for all their efforts.

Thanks also to Ali McKeown and Valerie Mitchell for their help.

My copy-editor, Polly Stupples performed a difficult task with diplomacy and thoroughness, in equal measure. She was the first person to cook an entire dinner party from the book, and cheered me enormously by her enthusiasm for the food.

I owe a debt of gratitude to Deborah Madison, the wonderful American cookery writer, whose influence the reader may detect within these pages. From her I learnt, among many other things worth knowing, that the most mundane of ingredients may indeed deserve a luxurious partner.

In the kitchen garden I have been greatly encouraged by the writing of Joy Larkcom. Her enthusiasm continues to inspire me to grow new things, and it is to her books that I turn with confidence, when gardening questions or problems arise.

Finally, my husband Andrew Ford both ate and test-cooked his way through virtually all the recipes with enormous patience, dedication and good humour. He frequently had to ask the question, 'What *was* I supposed to do with that onion?' and it never failed to make me smile. He held my hand through numerous crises, providing all manner of practical, technical and moral support throughout the entire process, and has been unfailingly kind and supportive. As if all that were not enough, he even contributed a couple of the (better) recipes.

# INTRODUCTION

Surely there has never been a better time to be vegetarian. New vegetables and fruits appear in a steady stream in our shops and supermarkets. Organic box schemes and farmers' markets are springing up everywhere; and for gardeners, heritage vegetable varieties – distributed through seed conservation programmes and specialist seed merchants – are enjoying a huge upsurge in popularity.

In modern vegetarian cookery a sense of cheerful eclecticism prevails. There are few long-standing traditions, so vegetarians feel free to cherry-pick from the multiplicity of cooking styles encountered. Most of us are quite adventurous about what we eat – the only rule is that it has to taste good. This makes for interesting and varied dining.

The recipes in this book are for people who enjoy food and cooking, but rarely want to spend hours in the kitchen. They are inspired by what is seasonally available, fresh and interesting. Rather than planning elaborate menus, I generally seek out what is looking good in the shops or garden, and cook accordingly.

Much of my cooking is inspired by what grows in the garden. I love being able to pick produce at the size I want it – usually small enough to need only minimal preparation and cooking – finger-sized golden courgettes to cook whole; baby runner beans small enough just to top and tail; tiny, delicate pink-striped beetroot, and so on. I would urge anyone who feels even half-way inclined to grow some of their own food. Start in a small way, with perhaps a few herbs, runner beans or strawberries, and enjoy them at their freshly-picked best. I certainly don't expect readers to become self-sufficient, but for the occasional vegetable or fruit you simply can't get in the shops – or for something I think is especially worth growing – I give a few horticultural pointers.

Much as I delight in the sensual aspects of food, I think it is vital not to lose sight of the fact that we eat in order to live. I want the food I eat to enhance my state of health, not diminish it, so I try to limit my intake of saturated fats and avoid food additives, pesticide residues, and all those other things I know or suspect don't do me much good. Based on that precautionary principle, my diet is almost entirely organic. There are plenty of things to eat which are both delicious *and* beneficial to health, and most of the recipes contained in this book fall into that category. Of course there are a few exceptions, and it will be obvious which they are, for those occasions when we feel the need to stray from the path of dietary righteousness!

## RECIPES SUITABLE FOR VEGANS

Vegans eat no animal products at all. This means no milk, butter, eggs, cheese, yogurt, honey, meat derivatives such as gelatine or rennet, or any manufactured food containing any of these items.

Many of my recipes are either suitable for vegans exactly as they stand, or can be adapted to be so with minimal alteration. In many cases, all you would need to do is substitute an extra tablespoon of olive oil for the small quantity of butter used in the initial sauté of vegetables. Vegan recipes are listed by category – vegan soups, vegan main courses, and so on – in the index and also highlighted in the table of contents.

## LOW FAT RECIPES

For those wishing to minimize fat consumption, low fat recipes are also listed by category in the index and highlighted in the table of contents.

# INGREDIENTS

My food philosophy is to use the best quality ingredients of their type. When I'm feeling broke, rather than settle for an inferior substitute, I prefer to use less of an ingredient, or to cook something different and intrinsically less expensive.

## OILS AND BUTTER

For most day to day cooking I use organic extra virgin olive oil. I don't see any point in economizing here, since I use so little anyway. Sometimes butter is needed to flavour a dish – again, I only use organic.

Where a very mild, neutral oil with minimal flavour is called for, peanut oil (often sold as groundnut oil) usually fits the bill, although it can occasionally be intense, depending on where it comes from. If you haven't used a particular brand before, have a good sniff before committing it to a sweet recipe. Sunflower oil is sometimes recommended as neutral, but can be overwhelmingly savoury and nutty. Certain dishes would be spoilt by the use of a too-obtrusive oil.

Nut oils like hazel or walnut are good in salad dressings, especially if you include a few of the corresponding nuts in the salad. They don't seem to cook well – I think they have a tendency to burn (something which is also true of sesame oil). Nut oils spoil quickly, so should be bought in small quantities and kept in the fridge. Generally the darker in colour, the less refined they are, and consequently the more flavour they have.

## VINEGARS

Can there still be anyone out there who has not been converted to balsamic vinegar? Its fruity, mild flavour is fantastic for salads, tomatoes, and a host of other things. It's my favourite vinegar for general use.

Where a delicate white wine vinegar is required, I frequently opt for Champagne vinegar. It is light and less astringent than many white wine vinegars, so if you need to substitute a different wine vinegar, reduce the amount and taste as you go.

In Chinese dishes and hybrid Asian-influenced stir-fries, dark, intense Chinese vinegar is preferable, but I've been known to use balsamic instead when I've run out. If you come across it (usually in Oriental food stores), it's worth buying a bottle – it's inexpensive and keeps for ages.

Japanese brown rice vinegar is what you need for sushi. It is cheap and readily available, so there's little point in substituting anything else.

Finally, for chips, there's no substitute for real malt vinegar.

WINE AND SPIRITS

I often use wine or other alcohol in cooking, particularly in the colder months. It can add depth and complexity to a dish and, especially in recipes which use very little fat, banishes any possible lingering sense of the penitential. If a recipe calls for red or white wine, I mean a reasonable dry table wine, unless otherwise stated. I don't think it's a good idea to put any wine in your food that you wouldn't be happy to drink.

I always keep a bottle of sweet Marsala for cooking, as it goes so well with so many foods, and I usually have brandy, kirsch and rum around for the same reason. A jar of rum-soaked raisins is another handy thing to have in the cupboard.

NUTS, AND HOW TO ROAST THEM

As will be apparent from even a cursory glance through this book, I use nuts frequently in cooking, but generally in small quantities for accent and textural contrast, rather than as a main ingredient. Nutritionally they are very concentrated, and a little goes a long way. In large amounts they can make for stodginess in a dish, which is not usually desirable. I buy nuts in small quantities frequently, and store them in their packets in an air-tight container, to minimize the likelihood of them going stale. Almonds and hazels I tend to buy ready-blanched, as it's a fiddle to do the job yourself.

I hardly ever use nuts without first roasting them, as it brings out the flavour immeasurably. It also makes them crisper. Even if they will be cooked again, as in a nut loaf or bread, I think they benefit from preliminary direct contact with oven heat. It is quite feasible to roast a batch in advance, cool them and simply put them back in the packet, and this is what I usually do.

The table below gives approximate timings in minutes for roasting whole nuts on the middle shelf of an oven pre-heated to 180°C (350°F, gas 4). You will need to adjust the temperature for fan ovens. Chopped nuts will cook more quickly.

|  | Light roast | Dark roast |
|---|---|---|
| Almonds | 10 | 13 |
| Cashews | 8 | 12 |
| Hazels | 8 | 12 |
| Macadamias | 9 | 12 |
| Pecans | 10 | 14 |
| Pine kernels | 5 | 7 |
| Walnuts | 9 | 12 |

Check the nuts frequently and don't let yourself be distracted – nuts have the capacity to burn very suddenly.

CHILLIES

Chilli peppers come in a vast array of strengths and colours. Often, the smaller ones are more fiery than the larger; however, the only foolproof way is to taste them, but carefully and in very small amounts. Some supermarkets now give an indication of strength on the label, which is helpful. My recipes generally use finely chopped fresh, rather than dried, chilli. The small flecks of bright colour do much more to enhance the appearance of the finished dish than does the rather murky brownish tinge of chilli powder, and the flavour is undoubtedly superior.

When preparing chillies, wear rubber gloves. It may be a little awkward, but is infinitely preferable to the stinging eyes (or other delicate bits!) that result from inadvertently wiping chilli juice onto a susceptible area. It is not sufficient to wash your hands after preparing them – the effect persists for a few hours. It is often more convenient to prepare a batch of fresh chillies all at once and freeze the surplus, as described on page 203.

GREEN VEGETABLES – STEAMING VERSUS BOILING

Greens cooked by steaming or boiling don't figure much in my culinary repertoire, but for a few specific recipes they are crucial. The choice between steaming or boiling presents me with a quandary. Steaming undoubtedly preserves nutrients better than boiling, but boiling preserves colour. Most green vegetables go a less than vibrant shade of olive if steamed, particularly if kept hanging around afterwards. Mostly I steam, but for recipes where the colour seems particularly important, or for entertaining, I boil! There are also health considerations regarding the rather generous use of salt in the boiling method described here.

To cook green vegetables in a way that preserves their colour, first bring a large pan of salted water to the boil – the addition of salt at 2 teaspoons per litre of water (1 teaspoon per pint) makes the water boil at a higher temperature, so the vegetables cook faster. Add the vegetables, cover the pan until the water comes back up to the boil, then remove the lid. Boil as fast as you dare (delicate vegetables like broccoli should be simmered), with the pan uncovered until the vegetables are tender but still have some bite. Drain them swiftly, and rinse briefly in cold water, before draining them again. Keeping the pan uncovered allows the enzymes responsible for discolouration to escape, and the brief rinse in cold water (known as refreshing) arrests the cooking process and sets the colour.

## CHEESES

Not all cheeses are strictly suitable for vegetarians, since some are set using animal rennet. The situation is further complicated by the fact that some cheeses made with vegetarian rennet are not actually labelled as such. If you buy from a good specialist cheese shop the proprietor may know what is what, otherwise you have no choice but to rely on the labelling.

## VEGETABLE STOCK

Vegetable stock presents something of a quandary. Making stock from scratch is a slow process, involving a lot of vegetable preparation. On the other hand, many stock cubes, powders, pastes, etc. are singularly revolting. They often contain food additives of dubious merit, so it's worth reading the small print before you buy. There are a few decent products on the UK market. The one I invariably come back to is Marigold Swiss Vegetable Bouillon, which is on sale in most health and whole food shops. It (like all the others I've tried) is quite salty, so taste the dish in which it is used, and add extra salt only if necessary. For those occasions when only the real thing will do, there is a reliable basic recipe on page 208.

# EQUIPMENT

You don't need cupboards full of kit to make the recipes in this book, but there are certain basic items I use continually and which I believe are worth serious investment.

## PANS

If you can possibly afford it, buy some decent pans. It will cause you financial pain, possibly severe, but will be worth it. Cheap pans are a false economy. It is better to have three or four really good solid ones than a dozen flimsy lightweights. I used heavy, professional-quality stainless steel pans while testing all the recipes. They will last a lifetime, are virtually indestructible and a joy to cook with. With stainless steel handles and lids, they can go in the oven or under the grill if necessary.

Not all stainless steel pans are the same. The best have a very heavy base, with a layer of copper sandwiched inside it to help conduct the heat. They will never buckle and, if burnt, can even be cleaned with a chisel and sandpaper – something I've had to do to mine on occasions. These pans conduct heat evenly and steadily. Food, even glutinous things like porridge, tends not to stick, so they are very easy to clean. Finally, any type of implement – metal, wood, whatever comes to hand – can be used with them. You are not restricted to those nasty nylon spatulas which melt if you leave them in the pan and are never thin enough to slide gracefully under the edge of a pancake or omelette.

## ROASTING TINS

I roast vegetables often, usually in a very large stainless steel roasting tin, which is almost as wide as my oven. Size matters, as vegetables roast better in a single layer, but the choice of material is not straightforward. Metal conducts heat better than glass or most ceramics, although stainless steel is not so good in this regard as ordinary steel. Ordinary steel rusts if left damp; enamel and non-stick coatings chip if you use metal cooking implements on them. I think stainless is the best compromise. I just wish I could find a huge stainless steel roasting tin with a well-fitting lid, as I seem to get through acres and acres of foil.

## KNIVES

Two knives are all I ever seem to need. A large cook's knife and a small paring knife. Again, it pays to invest in the best. Mine are stainless steel (including the handles), because I'm not always disciplined enough to dry them immediately after washing. If you buy really good ones they will be very sharp, will hold their sharpness for longer, and will be easier to re-sharpen when necessary. Cheaper knives blunt rapidly, and you will be forever sharpening them or cursing their bluntness. If you don't know how to do it, get a knowledgeable person at a specialist kitchen shop to show you the correct way to sharpen a knife using a steel. It is difficult to describe, but not to do.

Sharp knives are safer to use than blunt ones, so long as you treat them with respect. They will do the job more efficiently, with less effort and more control. This is especially useful when dealing with dense, hard-to-cut vegetables such as large pumpkins, swedes, celeriac, and so on.

Never put sharp knives in the dishwasher, always keep hold of the handles when they are in the washing up bowl concealed from view by soap suds, and dry and put them away immediately after washing. If you need to put a knife down while in use, get into the habit of laying it with the blade facing (and close to) the edge of the chopping board, or the back of the counter – that way you're less likely to pick it up by the sharp edge accidentally.

## FOOD PROCESSORS

Food processors take up a lot of space, but I think for someone who cooks frequently, they justify it. They need to be out and accessible, where they can be easily used, not lurking at the back of a cupboard. Mine gets used for making bread and biscuit crumbs, blending soups, grating cheese, making pastry, ice creams, and for umpteen other things, which would be possible but much slower by hand.

# SEED SUPPLIERS

Although most garden centres sell vegetable seeds their range is often rather limited. If you want to grow some of the more unusual items I mention, particularly the salad leaves, you will probably need to resort to mail order. The following seed merchants supply a wide range of interesting salad and vegetable seeds by post. Their catalogues make excellent reading.

Simpson's Seeds
The Walled Garden Nursery
Horningsham
Warminster
BA12 7NQ
01985 845004

Simpson's Seeds carry a wide range of unusual varieties of vegetable seeds, including a vast selection of tomatoes, many of which are not available elsewhere. They also sell young plants by mail order.

The Organic Gardening Catalogue
Riverdene Business Park
Molesey Road
Hersham
Surrey
KT12 4RG
01932 253666
www.organiccatalog.com

The Organic Gardening Catalogue lists a wide range of vegetable seeds, quite a few of which are organically raised, plus a comprehensive selection of gardening sundries geared specifically towards the organic gardener and grower.

Suffolk Herbs
Monks Farm
Coggeshall Road
Kelvedon
Essex
CO5 9PG
01376 572456
www.suffolkherbs.com

Suffolk Herbs have a good selection of seeds of oriental vegetables, herbs, western vegetables, grain crops, wild flowers, and a range of gardening sundries.

# STARTERS AND SOUPS

*I'm sure I can't be the only person who regularly finds restaurant starters more tempting than most of the main course offerings. Frequently I could happily dine on two or three starters and skip the main course entirely.*

*You could put together a few dishes from this chapter to serve as an informal supper. Alternatively some of the recipes that follow would happily stand alone for a light lunch, needing only a little salad, good bread and some fruit to make a complete meal, while in cold weather there is no more comforting lunch than a steaming, fragrant bowl of homemade soup.*

# PURÉE OF BROAD BEANS WITH FRESH TARRAGON

This pale green creamy purée – a dip for crisp, raw vegetables and bread sticks – is lovely as part of a mixed *hors d'œuvre*. Serve with one or two other dips – perhaps *Melitzanosalata* (see opposite) and *Fresh tomato and pepper salsa* (page 28) – and you have a nice, uncomplicated opener for a warm-weather dinner.

about 900 g (2 lb) fresh broad beans, prepared,
   or 300 g (10 oz) frozen
420 ml (15 fl oz) vegetable stock
1 clove of garlic, crushed
3 teaspoons lemon juice
2 tablespoons chopped fresh or frozen tarragon
$\frac{1}{2}$ level teaspoon sugar
salt and freshly ground black pepper

Simmer the beans in the vegetable stock until tender (3–10 minutes, depending on their age and size). Drain them, but save the stock. Place all the ingredients in a food processor and whiz until smooth, adding just enough of the stock to thin the purée to a manageable consistency. Taste, and adjust the seasoning as necessary. Although it can be chilled, the purée is rather good served freshly-made and lukewarm.

SERVES 4 WITH CRUDITÉS

# MELITZANOSALATA – GREEK AUBERGINE DIP

This is a wonderfully cool and refreshing dip for a summer's day. It is a good vehicle for crudités of raw vegetables, or would be equally at home with chunks of fresh baguette and a dish of fat, glossy Kalamata olives. The addition of a salad of luscious, sun-ripened tomatoes and salty, white feta cheese drizzled with green olive oil, and a bottle of ice-cold retsina would make for my perfect hot-weather lunch.

200 g (7 oz) full fat Greek cow's yogurt
1 large or 2 medium aubergines
1 clove garlic, crushed
2 tablespoons extra virgin olive oil
2 tablespoons white wine vinegar
salt and freshly ground black pepper

Oven temperature: 180°C (350°F, gas 4) – adjust for fan ovens

This dip should be quite solid and not at all watery, so the yogurt needs to be strained. Line a small colander or sieve either with a double layer of butter muslin or about four thicknesses of kitchen roll. Stand it over a bowl to catch any liquid that runs off. Pour off any water then tip the yogurt into the lined colander. Cover, and leave in the fridge for several hours, preferably overnight.

The aubergines are first baked until the flesh is soft. If they are reasonably small they could be grilled over a barbecue, after the heat has died down slightly, which would give them a good smoky flavour, but they are perfectly acceptable cooked in a normal domestic oven.

Whichever method you use, wash the aubergines and prick them all over with a fork, to prevent explosions. Assuming that you are using a normal domestic oven, heat it to a moderate temperature – around 180°C (350°F, gas 4), although the exact temperature is not critical – and bake the aubergines uncovered in a baking dish until they are very soft to the prod of a finger or blunt knife. This can take up to 1 hour, depending on their size. For smaller aubergines, start checking after 40 minutes.

Set aside the cooked aubergines until they are cool enough to handle, then cut them in half and scoop out the flesh. Put the flesh and all the other ingredients except the yogurt into a food processor and whiz until smooth. Scrape down any lumpy bits from the side of the bowl and whiz again, if necessary. Fold the strained yogurt gently into the aubergine mixture. Don't process after the yogurt has been added as it damages the structure. Taste, and adjust the seasoning, adding extra vinegar if necessary. Chill thoroughly before serving.

MAKES ABOUT 300 ML (10 FL OZ)

# MUSHROOMS STUFFED WITH ROQUEFORT AND WALNUTS

This recipe is lovely made with smaller field mushrooms in the autumn, if you know where to find them and can identify them safely. It's also fine using cultivated mushrooms with caps of about 5–6 cm (2 inch) diameter. Whether wild or tame, use the freshest mushrooms you can find – it really makes a difference in this recipe.

8–12 mushrooms, depending on size
1 clove garlic, crushed
100 g (3½ oz) Roquefort cheese
1 medium slice wholemeal bread
black pepper, freshly ground
1 tablespoon of finely chopped fresh parsley
60 g (2 oz) chopped walnuts
a little butter
lemon wedges, to serve

Heat the oven to its hottest setting – around 250°C (475°F, gas 9).

Clean the mushrooms and remove the stalks. Put the stalks, garlic, cheese, bread, pepper and parsley in the food processor and whiz briefly. Stir in the walnuts by hand, to keep their texture.

Pile this mixture into the mushroom caps and set them on a baking tray that has been lightly buttered. If you have some of those little individual cast iron baking dishes, by all means use them.

Bake the mushrooms uncovered for about 8 minutes, and serve while they are still sizzling, with a wedge of lemon and some decent bread.

SERVES 4

# FIELD MUSHROOMS STUFFED WITH HAZELNUTS AND TORTA DI DOLCELATTE

Torta di Dolcelatte is a luscious Italian cheese comprising thin, alternating layers of blue-veined Dolcelatte interleaved with creamy Mascarpone. Always well-flavoured but never astringent, it is usually easy to find, but if you have problems, just mix equal quantities of Mascarpone (or other cream cheese) with Dolcelatte.

If you can't get field mushrooms this dish is fine made with some of the larger flat mushrooms to be had in the shops.

**4 huge or 8 medium-sized field mushrooms**
**30 g (1 oz) butter**
**1 tablespoon olive oil**
**4 tablespoons finely-chopped shallots**
**2 garlic cloves, crushed**
**110 g (4 oz) Torta di Dolcelatte cheese**
**4 teaspoons lemon juice**
**60 g (2 oz) hazelnuts, roasted and coarsely chopped**

Oven temperature: 200°C (400°F, gas 6) – adjust for fan ovens

Clean and de-stalk the mushrooms. If you can get away with just wiping them with a damp cloth, so much the better.

Trim the stalks and chop them finely.

Melt the butter and oil together in a small pan and brush a little of the mixture over the mushroom caps. Place the mushrooms on an oven-proof baking tray or dish, and set on one side.

Sauté the shallots, mushroom stalks and garlic in the remaining oil and butter mixture, over a moderate heat until soft. Remove the pan from the heat and stir in all the remaining ingredients with a fork.

Pile the filling on the mushrooms, spreading it out so the entire surface is covered.

Bake, uncovered, for about 10 minutes in the pre-heated oven.

SERVES 4

# SUSHI ROLLS

Sushi rolls look impressive, are very low in fat and are really quite easy to make. So long as you stick to vegetable-only fillings as given here, they are also vegan. A special bamboo rolling mat is a help but not essential – the same effect can be achieved with a clean tea-towel folded in half, or a large linen napkin.

Although it's OK to make them in advance, don't serve sushi straight from the fridge. They need to be at room temperature, as ice-cold sticky rice is clammy and unappealing.

SUSHI ROLLS

250 g (9 oz) sushi rice (short-grained white rice)
400 ml (14 fl oz) water
1½ level teaspoons salt
40 g (1½ oz) sugar
3 tablespoons Japanese rice vinegar
3 sheets sushi nori (Japanese culinary seaweed)
filling: for suggestions see below

DIPPING SAUCE

3 tablespoons Japanese rice vinegar
3 tablespoons shoyu or tamari
1 level teaspoon prepared wasabi (Japanese horseradish) paste
2 level teaspoons sugar
2 tablespoons cold water

TO SERVE

a small pack of sliced pickled ginger (optional but nice)

Cook the rice with the water and salt at a gentle simmer (lowest possible heat) in a covered pan for 20 minutes. Take it off the heat and let it stand for 10 minutes more with the lid on the pan, by which time all the water should have been absorbed. Stir in the sugar and rice vinegar gently using a fork.

Take a nori sheet and place it on the bamboo mat, napkin or whatever you are using. Spread one third of the rice evenly over the nori (pay particular attention to the sides), leaving a 2 cm (1 inch) strip of nori uncovered at the end furthest away from you, for sealing purposes. With the back of a teaspoon, make a shallow linear depression in the rice, parallel to the 'sealing strip', but about one third of the way in from the opposite end. Arrange your chosen filling evenly along this depression, then, using the mat or napkin to support it, roll up the nori, working away from yourself, as tightly and evenly as you can. Dampen the bare strip of nori with a little cold water to get a good seal.

Keep the rolls intact until just before serving. They can be wrapped in cling-film and refrigerated for up to 48 hours, if necessary. Cut into 2 cm (1 inch) slices with a very sharp knife, moistened with cold water. You'll probably need to clean the knife between slices. Discard the ragged end slices.

THE DIPPING SAUCE

Combine the ingredients for the dipping sauce thoroughly. Make sure the wasabi paste is well mixed in as it's incredibly hot if you accidentally get a lump!

Arrange the sushi slices on a large platter but serve individual portions of pickled ginger and dipping sauce in tiny bowls or ramekins.

SERVES 6

SUGGESTED FILLINGS

When steaming vegetables to use as sushi filling cook them for the absolute minimum time needed. They should just have the raw edge taken off, but still be a very long way from soggy. The times given below are my best estimates for individual vegetables, but you should test as you go, since it's very easy to over-cook them.

- Long batons of steamed carrot (3 minutes) and green courgettes (2 minutes, use pieces with some skin attached) laid side by side to give a two-colour effect when the roll is sliced.
- Long strips of steamed red, green and yellow pepper (2 minutes), laid side by side, for a three-colour effect.
- Cut long cylinders of pumpkin flesh using an apple-corer, and steam for no more than 4 minutes. Refresh immediately in cold water, then drain and dry them on kitchen paper.
- Asparagus – the cooking time is very variable according to its age and thickness, so just test as you go, and don't let it get limp!

# FRESH TOMATO AND PEPPER SALSA

Hot, raw and invigorating, this lively salsa could not be simpler. The proportions are not critical, but it's a good idea to stick to about two parts tomato to one part sweet pepper, by volume.

The amount of chilli included depends on the ferocity of the particular chillies used (they vary enormously) and, of course, personal preference. When handling chillies I suggest wearing rubber gloves, since any juice on the fingers is easily transferred to eyes or other delicate skin, with painful results. This can happen several hours after your hands have been in contact with the chillies, even after washing. It is worth chopping the chillies and garlic quite finely, to eliminate the risk of large chunks escaping the food processor blades.

2 or 3 medium-sized unpeeled ripe tomatoes, coarsely chopped
1 small or ½ a large sweet red pepper, de-seeded and coarsely chopped
1 clove of garlic, peeled and finely chopped
½ a small red onion, chopped (more, if you like it)
a generous bunch fresh coriander leaves, washed and de-stalked
1 tablespoon olive oil
salt, to taste
a few drops of fresh lime juice
between ½ and 2 fresh red chillies (see above) – de-seeded and finely chopped

Put all the ingredients in a food processor and whiz briefly (use the pulse setting), so that some texture is retained. Stir the salsa just before serving as it tends to separate out a little, but don't leave it sitting around for too long or it will lose its freshness.

Serve with Margaritas and tortilla chips as an appetizer, or as part of a Mexican main course with tortillas, *Refritos* (page 92) and *Guacamole* (page 54).

VARIATION
Use yellow tomatoes and/or peppers to vary the colour-scheme.

SERVES 4

# TOMATO TARTLETS WITH CRISP PARMESAN TOPPING

I cook these little tartlets in the type of deep metal baking tins used for mince pies. Small cake tins are often too shallow – you need enough depth, at least 2 cm (1 inch), to hold a reasonable amount of filling. If necessary, cook in a large tart tin for slightly longer than specified below and cut into wedges. To prevent the pastry cases collapsing during blind baking, sit a lightly-oiled, spare, matching baking tin on top of the pastry as it cooks.

Don't be tempted to eat the tartlets straight from the oven, as the flavour doesn't develop until they have cooled slightly. Similarly, don't serve them chilled. They should be just warm, or at room temperature.

THE PASTRY

1 batch of *Cheese pastry* (page 162)

THE FILLING

2 large eggs
3 tablespoons double cream
100 g (3½ oz) concentrated tomato purée
2–3 tablespoons finely sliced chives, welsh onions or spring onions
40 g (1½ oz) finely grated fresh Parmesan cheese
salt and freshly ground black pepper

THE TOPPING

30 g (1 oz) fresh wholewheat bread-crumbs
15 g (½ oz) fresh Parmesan cheese, finely grated

Oven temperature: 200°C (400°F, gas 6) – adjust for fan ovens

Make the cheese pastry according to the instructions on page 162 and put it to rest in the fridge while you prepare the filling.

For the filling, beat the eggs lightly with a fork and stir in the remaining ingredients until thoroughly combined. If using spring onions, be sure to include plenty of the green part.

Combine the bread-crumbs and grated Parmesan cheese for the topping, and set aside for later.

Roll out the pastry thinly on a floured work surface and line the tart tins (there is no need to oil the tins). Prick over the base of each pastry case with a fork, and brush with some of the lightly beaten egg white left over from pastry-making. You can add the remains of this egg white to the tart filling, if you like. Bake the pastry cases for 10 minutes, then take them out of the oven and turn the heat down to 180°C (350°F, gas 4) – adjust for fan ovens.

Spoon the filling into the pastry cases, and sprinkle on some of the topping mixture, leaving a small bare margin around the edge of each tartlet. Bake for a further 10–15 minutes, until the tartlets are firm in the centre and the topping crisp and brown.

MAKES 20 TARTLETS

# MUSHROOM AND AUBERGINE WONTONS

Wontons are little squares, usually about 10 cm (4 inches), of thin pastry, available frozen from Chinese shops and some of the better supermarkets. They are filled with something intensely savoury – traditionally seafood or meat – but here with a mixture of vegetables with hot and sour seasoning, and are then either steamed or deep-fried. They make a good *hors d'œuvre* served with *Sweet chilli dipping sauce* (page 190).

If you want to steam them I recommend using Chinese bamboo steamers. They're not only less expensive but more practical than most of the western types, and look nice enough to take to the table. They are designed as tiers that can be stacked on top of each other in a wok or large frying pan, over a simmering pool of water, with a lid on the top tier to contain the steam.

If you want to make fried wontons and can't find the authentic wonton dough, a double layer of filo pastry cut into squares makes a reasonable substitute, but it won't stand up to steaming.

### THE PASTRY
1 packet frozen wonton pastries, defrosted
a little flour, to stop the pastry sticking

### THE VEGETABLES
1 medium aubergine, washed and cut into 5 mm (¼ inch) cubes
salt
2 tablespoons sunflower or groundnut oil
1 small onion, peeled and finely chopped
a piece of fresh ginger about the size of 2 garlic cloves, peeled and finely chopped
110 g (4 oz) mushrooms, cleaned and finely chopped
1 clove of garlic, peeled and finely chopped
2 tablespoons chopped fresh coriander leaf

### THE SEASONING
1 level teaspoon cornflour
1 level teaspoon sugar
3 tablespoons natural soy sauce
3 tablespoons of rice wine or dry sherry
1 teaspoon dark Chinese vinegar (balsamic would do at a pinch)
1 fresh red chilli, de-seeded and finely chopped

Sprinkle the aubergine lightly but evenly with salt and leave it in a colander over a bowl for about 30 minutes, then rinse and drain it. Heat the oil in a heavy, shallow pan with a well-fitting lid. Sauté the onions, aubergine and ginger for a few minutes, stirring. Cover the pan, reduce the heat, and cook gently for about 5–6 minutes, stirring occasionally.

While the aubergine is cooking, mix all the seasoning ingredients together in a bowl or jug. It is easier to do this if you put the cornflour and sugar in first and add the liquids gradually, stirring after each addition.

When the aubergine is quite soft, remove the pan lid, add the mushrooms and garlic, turn the heat up slightly and stir. Give the seasoning liquid a last-minute stir, then tip it into the pan with the vegetables. Cook, stirring, with the pan uncovered, until the aubergine is tender, virtually all the liquid has evaporated and the mixture is quite dry. Add the chopped coriander leaf at the end of the cooking time. Allow the filling to cool a little before attempting to fill the wontons.

ASSEMBLY

Keeping the unused pile of wonton pastry covered with polythene or foil, take individual squares of pastry and place a scant tablespoonful of filling in the centre. Gather up the edges of the pastry and pinch them together firmly around the filling, excluding as much air as possible. The shape you should be aiming for is that of an old-fashioned, spherical Christmas pudding gathered up in a cloth. Don't be too generous with the filling, as this makes the wontons more likely to disintegrate during cooking. Place the little parcels on a floured plate or baking sheet until you've finished making them, but don't leave them sitting around for too long as the filling may seep and make them soggy.

DIGRESSION – THE SPRING ROLL OPTION

If you find making the wonton parcels too much of a fiddle or just fancy a change, the pastries can be used to make mini spring rolls. Place a line of filling along one side of the pastry square and roll up, tucking the ends in securely as you go to avoid leaks. Seal the pastry with a little cold water applied with your finger tip, then fry the spring rolls as described below. If you have to use filo instead of wontons this option works better than the 'Christmas pudding' method.

TO FRY

Deep-fry the wontons a few at a time in hot oil for a couple of minutes until they turn crisp and golden. Drain them well and blot with kitchen paper. Cooked in this way they can be served hot or at room temperature. If it's more convenient to cook them in advance, they can be re-heated in a warm oven for 5–10 minutes.

TO STEAM

Place the wontons in a steamer, sitting each one on a small square of non-stick baking parchment (to prevent them sticking to the steamer). Cover with a lid and steam over boiling water for about 8 minutes, then serve immediately.

SERVES 4

# SOUPS – SOME GROUND RULES FOR IMPROVISATION

To make a smooth, creamy soup you generally start by sautéing the vegetables in a little olive oil or butter, or a mixture of the two. Adding oil to the butter prevents it from burning. Usually, you will need onions and perhaps garlic, with whatever other vegetable you want to use. Unless you're deliberately setting out to make a mixed vegetable soup, it's probably better to stick to one main vegetable ingredient. That way your soup will taste of something definite and identifiable. If you want quite a thick soup, add peeled, diced potato at this stage. One large or two to three small potatoes will be enough for most recipes – too many and you end up with something resembling wallpaper paste!

Anyone trying to minimize fat intake may omit the sautéing stage entirely and just simmer the vegetables in stock. It doesn't make much discernible difference to the end result.

After the initial sauté, pour in just enough vegetable stock to cover the vegetables and simmer, with a lid on the pan, until the vegetables are tender. Depending on the vegetables chosen and the size to which you've cut them, this will take between twenty and forty minutes. For a cream soup the vegetables need to be very tender – this is not the time for cooking them *al dente*.

Purée the cooked vegetables and stock in a food processor or blender. The texture can be varied by leaving some of the vegetable chunks whole. Appropriate fresh or frozen herbs can be added at this stage. Most herbs do not benefit from being cooked and are best added near the end of the process. The herb leaves should be washed and can be put in the food processor whole – they'll get chopped during the blending. Return the soup to the pan for re-heating, finishing and final adjustment of seasonings.

Add more stock or milk if the soup is too thick. Stir in some cream if you want to make the texture more velvety. To make a creamy soup without using dairy products, use creamed coconut, chopped and stirred into the hot soup just before serving. It is as well to test a couple of times as you gradually add the coconut – the flavour should not be overwhelming. Coconut adds a slight sweetness, which you may want to counterbalance with a touch of lemon juice or vinegar.

I generally make soup with Marigold Swiss Vegetable Bouillon Powder, rather than home-made stock, but if you want to make your own there is a good general purpose recipe on page 208. The stock powder is quite salty, so if using it, don't add extra salt without first tasting.

Some of the following recipes make quite large quantities of soup, often enough for 6–8 servings. This is deliberate, since it's virtually as easy to make a lot as a little, and soup generally keeps very well in the fridge for a few days. Many of the soups also freeze successfully (in individual portions for maximum flexibility) and make a welcome quick snack.

# SPICED CREAM OF PUMPKIN SOUP WITH SEVILLE ORANGE

This soup is flavoured with tangy, bitter Seville oranges – the kind used for marmalade – a fantastic and much under-used ingredient. They are only available for a short time in the middle of winter, so if you can't get them use a little lemon juice instead.

The smoked paprika also falls into the category of very nice but not absolutely essential. You can often find it in the specialist ingredients section of major supermarkets, and if you see it I'd urge you to buy some. It has a wonderful and distinctive aroma, and a little goes a long way.

Any type of pumpkin or winter squash may be used.

700 to 900 g (1½ to 2 lb) pumpkin flesh (buy about a third extra to allow for
    wastage)
2 tablespoons olive oil
1 large or 2 small onions, chopped
1 potato, peeled and diced
3 stalks of celery, sliced
4 cloves of garlic, peeled and chopped
1 teaspoon chopped sage leaves
1 teaspoon chopped thyme leaves
1 teaspoon smoked paprika
1 litre (2 pints) vegetable stock
grated rind and juice of 2 Seville oranges (or the juice of half a lemon)
60 g (2 oz) creamed coconut
salt and freshly ground black pepper
1 or 2 teaspoons of sugar if necessary
fresh snipped chives
swirl of crème fraîche to garnish (omit for vegans)

Either peel and dice the pumpkin (an easy method of doing this is given in the *Pumpkin risotto* recipe on page 98) or, if you have the oven on for something else, halve, de-seed, and bake the pumpkin cut sides down on an oiled tray in the oven until tender.

Heat the oil in a large soup pan, add the vegetables (raw pumpkin, onions, celery, garlic and potato), sage, thyme and paprika, and fry, stirring, over a moderate heat for a few minutes. Pour in the stock and bring the soup to the boil. Cover the pan and simmer until the vegetables are completely tender – about 20–30 minutes. If using pre-baked pumpkin, scoop out the flesh and add it to the pan towards the end of the cooking time.

Purée the soup in a food processor or blender in batches and return it to the pan to re-heat. Add the orange rind and juice, stir in the creamed coconut, and adjust the seasoning if necessary. It may need a little sugar to correct the acidity. If it seems too thick, add a little more hot vegetable stock (or milk for non-vegans).

Serve out the soup and garnish each portion with crème fraîche and chives.

SERVES 4 FOR LUNCH, 6 AS A STARTER

# LOVAGE SOUP

Lovage is a herb you are unlikely to find fresh on the supermarket shelves. I don't know why, because it has a terrific, intense celery flavour and is very easy indeed to grow, much easier than basil, for instance. Do not be alarmed at reports of its vast size. It can easily be kept within bounds by frequent picking. Indeed, the leaves should be picked young, ideally when they are about 15 cm (6 inches) long, and certainly before they become large and coarse. They freeze well (which is worth doing, if only so that you can make this lovely soup in the winter months) and the frequent picking encourages the plant to produce more. One plant is ample for the average household.

This soup, comfort food *par excellence*, is delicious served with hot garlic or herb bread; see *Herb butters* (page 205).

Thanks to my husband Andrew for this particular incarnation of the recipe – his inclusion of carrot and egg yolk gives the soup a beautiful delicate golden glow.

2 large onions, peeled and chopped
1 large carrot, peeled and chopped
1 large or 2 medium potatoes, peeled and chopped
½ a head of celery, washed and sliced
2 tablespoons of olive oil
500 ml (18 fl oz) vegetable stock
handful of young lovage leaves, washed and de-stalked (about 15–20 g)
100 ml (4 fl oz) cream
100 ml (4 fl oz) milk
2 egg yolks
salt and freshly ground black pepper

Sauté all the vegetables (onions, carrots, potato and celery) in the olive oil for a few minutes. Pour in the vegetable stock. Bring to the boil, turn down to a simmer, put a lid on the pan and cook for about 30 minutes, until the vegetables are tender.

Put the lovage leaves in the food processor or blender and whiz the soup with them, in batches if necessary. In the last batch, add the milk, cream and egg yolks. Put it all back in the rinsed-out pan and re-heat gently, adding salt and pepper to taste. Don't let it boil, or the egg yolks will curdle.

SERVES 3 FOR LUNCH, 4 OR 5 AS A STARTER

# CREAM OF CAULIFLOWER SOUP WITH WALNUTS

A pale, wintery soup with a smooth and luxurious texture. If you want to make this in advance don't add the parsley until just before serving. If you do the colour will deteriorate, although it will still taste perfectly fine.

1–2 tablespoons olive oil
1 large onion, chopped
2–3 stalks celery, chopped
1 large or 2–3 small potatoes, peeled and diced
1 cauliflower, chopped
1 clove garlic, chopped
1 litre (2 pints) vegetable stock
a handful of fresh parsley
150 ml (5 fl oz) single cream (vegans substitute 60 g (2 oz) creamed coconut)
salt and freshly ground black pepper
scant handful of roasted walnuts, chopped finely (see page 16 for roasting times)

Heat the oil in a large pan. Add the onion, celery, potatoes and cauliflower and sauté for 2–3 minutes, then add the garlic, followed by the stock. Bring to the boil, lower the heat to a simmer, and cook gently with a lid on the pan for about 20 minutes, until everything is tender.

Place the washed but un-chopped parsley leaves in the food processor. When the soup vegetables are cooked, ladle them (plus their cooking liquid) into the processor on top of the parsley. Whiz until smooth and cream in colour, lightly flecked with specks of bright green. You will probably need to do this in more than one batch. Rinse out the pan and return all the soup to it.

Re-heat the soup, taste, and adjust the seasoning, adding salt and pepper if needed. Add the cream or creamed coconut, and heat the soup without boiling it. Thin with a little more stock or milk, if necessary. Stir in the chopped walnuts at the very last minute before serving so they retain their crispness. Alternatively, scatter a few on the top of each individual portion before you take the soup to the table.

SERVES 4 FOR LUNCH, 6 AS A STARTER

# CAULIFLOWER AND POTATO SOUP WITH INDIAN SPICES

This recipe makes enough soup for around 10 servings. It freezes well, but is also quite easy to reduce down to half quantity if this is too much. It is very much a winter soup and virtually a meal in itself.

4 level teaspoons coriander seeds
2 level teaspoons cumin seeds
8 cloves of garlic, peeled and coarsely chopped
90 g (3 oz) piece of fresh ginger, peeled and coarsely chopped
1 fresh chilli, de-seeded and chopped
2 medium onions
4 tablespoons olive or sunflower oil
1 level teaspoon ground turmeric
1 kg (2 lb) potatoes, peeled and diced into 2 cm (1 inch) cubes
3 medium tomatoes, peeled and chopped
2 level teaspoons garam masala
freshly ground black pepper
3 tablespoons lemon juice
4 level teaspoons salt
1 huge or 2 medium cauliflowers, cut into small florets
200 g (7 oz) creamed coconut, cut into chunks
4 tablespoons coriander leaves, chopped

Toast the coriander seeds in a dry saucepan over a medium heat, until they start to go slightly brown. Transfer them to a grinder or mortar. Toast the cumin seeds similarly (use the same pan), then add to the grinder. Grind the seeds together, finely. Put the garlic, ginger, chilli and onions in a food processor or blender. Whiz to a paste with a few tablespoons of water.

Heat the oil in your largest pan, and fry the paste, ground seeds and turmeric for a few minutes. Add the potatoes, tomatoes, garam masala, pepper, lemon juice and salt to the pan. Stir well, add enough water to just cover the vegetables, bring the pan to the boil, reduce the heat, cover, and simmer for 10 minutes.

Add the prepared cauliflower, plus extra water if necessary, just enough to cover the vegetables. Simmer for a further 10 minutes or so, just until the cauliflower is barely tender. If you want to freeze the soup, the cauliflower should be slightly crisper than if it is to be consumed immediately.

Put the coconut into the food processor, add a few ladles of the soup and the coriander leaves, and whiz. Stir this back into the soup pan. You can purée all the soup, but I think it is better with some texture.

SERVES 6 FOR LUNCH, 10 AS A STARTER

# CARROT AND CORIANDER SOUP

Although this soup is available at chill counters everywhere, this home made version really is much nicer. It is simple to make, and costs next to nothing.

1 large onion
1 kg (2 lb) carrots
1 medium-sized potato
2 tablespoons olive oil
2 cloves of garlic
2 cm (1 inch) cube of fresh ginger
600 ml (1 pint) vegetable stock
150 ml (5 fl oz) single cream (vegans substitute 60 g (2 oz) creamed coconut)
juice of half a lemon
salt and freshly ground black pepper
about 15 g (½ oz) fresh coriander leaves, washed, de-stalked and chopped

Peel and roughly chop the onion, carrots and potato and fry them gently in the olive oil, in a large pan, stirring from time to time.

Peel and finely chop the garlic and ginger, and add them to the pan. Add the vegetable stock, cover the pan, and simmer for 25–30 minutes, until all the vegetables are tender.

Purée the soup, in batches if necessary, in a food processor or blender, then return it to the rinsed out pan and re-heat gently.

Stir in the cream (or creamed coconut) and lemon juice, taste, and add salt and pepper if necessary. Make sure the soup does not boil or the cream may curdle.

Just before serving, stir in most of the chopped coriander leaves, leaving a few to scatter decoratively on top for a garnish.

SERVES 3 FOR LUNCH, 5 AS A STARTER

# CELERY AND CELERIAC SOUP WITH FENNEL

Celeriac, with its knobbly, unprepossessing exterior, may lack the immediate visual appeal of many other vegetables, but has ample culinary compensations. It combines the texture and colour of parsnips with an intense celery flavour, and is one of my favourite vegetables. There's no denying it's an awkward shape – you just have to resign yourself to the fact that there will be a lot of wastage during preparation and consign the parings to the compost heap.

The celery imparts a delicate pale green tinge to the soup which looks pretty, especially when flecked with bright green parsley, added just before serving. The soup will be suitable for vegans if you omit the butter (add an extra tablespoon of olive oil instead) and finish it with creamed coconut rather than dairy cream.

2 tablespoons olive oil
15 g (½ oz) butter (vegans substitute extra oil)
1 large onion, peeled and chopped
3 level teaspoons dried fennel seeds
1 large head of celery – cleaned, trimmed and chopped
1 large celeriac root
1 large potato, peeled and diced
juice of 1 lemon
up to 2 litres (3½ pints) vegetable stock
100 g (4 oz) creamed coconut (for vegans) or 150 ml (5 fl oz) double cream
salt and freshly ground black pepper
3 tablespoons finely chopped parsley
fresh fennel fronds for garnish (optional)

Warm the oil and butter in a large soup pan, and fry the onion, fennel seeds and celery gently for a few minutes, stirring occasionally, until the onion starts to brown slightly.

While the onion and celery are cooking, prepare the celeriac. Have a large bowl of cold water ready, and as you peel and dice the celeriac, put it immediately into the water. If you leave its cut surfaces exposed to air they will turn brown, spoiling the colour, although not the flavour, of the finished soup.

Add the potato, the drained celeriac and lemon juice to the soup pan, followed by sufficient vegetable stock just to cover the other ingredients. Cover the pan and simmer for about 30 minutes until the vegetables are very tender.

Purée the soup in batches, then return it to the rinsed-out pan. Dilute with some of the remaining vegetable stock if the soup is too thick. Add the roughly chopped creamed coconut or double cream and re-heat, stirring, but don't allow the soup to boil. Taste and add salt if needed, plus a generous grinding of black pepper. Just before serving stir in the chopped parsley. Garnish each serving with a tiny frond of fresh fennel, if you have any.

ABOUT 8 SERVINGS

# CREAM OF JERUSALEM ARTICHOKE SOUP

Jerusalem artichokes are relatively cheap to buy and, while slightly more of a fiddle to prepare than potatoes, which they resemble, are much less hassle than their 'globe' namesakes. The flavour is quite unlike anything else. I like it enormously, but it is distinctive enough to not be universally popular. Sadly they have a reputation for being indigestible, but this can be partially countered by cooking them with ginger, fennel or caraway seeds.

This is a lovely, savoury but delicate, pale soup for winter. Its creamy, unctuous texture flatters the sweet and slightly nutty flavour of the artichokes.

1 kg (2 lb) Jerusalem artichokes
1 tablespoon lemon juice
thumb-sized piece of fresh ginger, peeled and finely chopped
2 medium onions, peeled and chopped
3 level teaspoons dried fennel seeds
1 tablespoon olive oil
4 stalks celery, chopped
350 g (12 oz) potatoes, peeled and diced
1 litre (2 pints) vegetable stock
small bunch of parsley (4–5 branches)
a few chives
60–90 ml (2–3 fl oz) double cream
milk to thin (optional)
1 teaspoon Champagne vinegar or fresh lemon juice

Peel and chop the artichokes, dropping them as you cut them into a bowl of cold water to which the lemon juice has been added. This prevents the cut surfaces from browning.

Sauté the ginger, onions and fennel seeds in the olive oil in a large soup pot over a moderate heat. When the onions start to colour slightly add the celery, potatoes and drained artichokes. Pour in the stock, bring it up to the boil, cover the pan and simmer gently for 20–25 minutes, until the vegetables are very soft.

Purée the hot soup in a blender or food processor, adding the parsley leaves and chives so they get finely chopped. Rinse out the pan, return the soup to it, and re-heat. Stir in the cream, and thin with a little milk or water if it is too thick for your taste, making sure the soup does not boil. Check the seasoning and adjust if necessary. Stir in the Champagne vinegar, which should be just enough to brighten the delicate flavour without being obtrusive.

SERVES 6 AS A STARTER, 4 FOR LUNCH

# SIMPLE WINTER VEGETABLE SOUP

In this recipe, some of the soup is puréed after cooking to thicken the base liquid, and then stirred back into the pan, giving a hearty soup with plenty of texture. I like to be able to see and taste the separate ingredients; however, if you prefer a smooth soup, simply purée the whole lot in batches.

Note: when preparing celeriac, put the pieces into cold water immediately, as the cut surfaces discolour if exposed to air.

1 tablespoon olive oil
2 onions, peeled and chopped
2 cloves garlic, peeled and finely chopped
½ medium celeriac root, peeled and diced
1 leek, cleaned and sliced
2 stalks celery, cleaned and sliced
3 medium carrots, peeled and sliced
1 parsnip, peeled and diced
1 potato, peeled and diced
1 litre (2 pints) vegetable stock
2 or 3 stalks of fresh parsley
150 ml (5 fl oz) single cream (vegans substitute 60 g (2 oz) creamed coconut)
salt and freshly ground black pepper

Warm the olive oil in a large, heavy pan. Sauté all the vegetables (onions, garlic, celeriac, leeks, celery, carrots, parsnip and potato) in the olive oil for a few minutes. Add the stock, bring the soup to the boil, put a lid on the pan, and simmer for 20–25 minutes, until the vegetables are very tender.

Put the parsley leaves in the food processor bowl, add a generous ladle of the soup mixture, and process until smooth. Stir this mixture back into the soup. Add the cream or creamed coconut, and re-heat. If the soup seems too thick, add a little more hot water or vegetable stock. Taste, and add salt and pepper if necessary.

This soup could be served with parsley-flavoured *Herb dumplings* (page 43).

SERVES 4 FOR LUNCH, 6 AS A STARTER

# SPINACH AND POTATO SOUP WITH INDIAN SPICES

I like to make this spicy, aromatic soup for a winter lunch. The potato makes it quite substantial and chilli heat keeps out the cold.

2 tablespoons olive oil
2 onions, peeled and coarsely chopped
6 cloves of garlic, peeled and chopped
2 cm (1 inch) piece of fresh ginger, peeled and finely chopped
2 level tablespoons ground cumin seed
2 level tablespoons ground coriander seed
1 fresh hot red chilli, de-seeded and finely chopped
2 tablespoons tomato purée
500 g (1 lb) potatoes, peeled and cut into 1 cm (½ inch) cubes
600 ml (1 pint) vegetable stock
salt and freshly ground black pepper
500 g (1 lb) spinach, washed, picked over and chopped
juice of half a lemon
800 ml (28 fl oz) coconut milk (canned is fine)
pinch or two of sugar (optional)
fresh coriander leaves to garnish

When preparing the chilli remember to wear rubber gloves as the juice can sting sensitive skin fiercely for up to several hours after the hands have been in contact with it, even after repeated washing.

In a large pan (minimum capacity 3½ litres – 6½ pints) heat the olive oil over a low heat. Put the onion in the pan and let it sweat gently as you prepare the other ingredients. Next add the garlic, ginger, cumin seeds, coriander seeds, chilli and tomato purée. Cook for a few minutes more, giving the pan a stir from time to time.

Add the potatoes, 1 teaspoon salt and the stock. Bring the pan to the boil, cover and simmer for 15 minutes, then add the spinach. Squash it down firmly so it will fit in the pan – when cooked it will reduce considerably in volume. Put the lid on the pan and let the spinach wilt in the steam for a few minutes, then stir it into the soup and simmer for 5 minutes more until the potatoes are well cooked.

Purée about half the cooked vegetables, then stir them back into the pan.

Re-heat the soup, adding the lemon juice and coconut milk. Taste for seasoning and add more salt, pepper and lemon juice if necessary. Serve garnished with a generous sprinkling of chopped coriander leaves.

SERVES 5 FOR LUNCH, 8 AS A STARTER

# CREAM OF TOMATO SOUP WITH BASIL

Although this soup is very simple, it can be quite sublime, given some really good tomatoes. I like to make it towards the end of summer, when I have a glut of tomatoes in the garden that have ripened in the sun on the vine. Actually, it's even better in the cold dark days of January, made from those same sun-ripened tomatoes out of the freezer, when just the scent of it is enough to transport you instantly to a balmy August afternoon . . .

I believe the tomatoes need peeling for this recipe, but I can never bring myself to de-seed them. It seems to me that most of their flavour is in the juicy flesh surrounding the seeds, and if keeping the seeds means a small compromise on texture, then so be it. If it bothers you, put the soup through a sieve.

15 g (½ oz) butter
3 medium sized onions, peeled and chopped
2–3 smallish potatoes, peeled and chopped
2 kg (4 lb) ripe tomatoes, peeled and chopped
5 cloves garlic, peeled and chopped
2 bay leaves
salt and freshly ground black pepper
bunch of fresh basil, weighing about 15 g (½ oz), washed and de-stalked
200 ml (6 fl oz) single cream
milk to thin

In a large pan, melt the butter and sauté the onions gently for a few minutes, allowing them to brown just a little. Add the potatoes, tomatoes, garlic, bay leaves and 1 heaped teaspoon of salt. Bring it all to the boil, stirring, then reduce the heat, cover the pan, and simmer for about 25–30 minutes until everything is disintegrating and soft. Meanwhile put the basil leaves into the food processor bowl.

Remove the bay leaves, then process the soup with the basil leaves, until smooth. You will probably need to do this in two or three batches. Rinse out the pan then return the soup to it, stir well and re-heat. Pour in the cream and add milk to thin it to the desired consistency. Don't let it boil. Add some freshly ground black pepper, taste, and add more salt if necessary.

This is very good served with hot *Pesto bread* (page 198).

VARIATIONS

- This soup is also nice if left chunky, in which case grate rather than chop the potato to thicken the soup.
- Use fresh mint instead of basil, and serve the soup with garlic rather than pesto bread.

SERVES 4 FOR LUNCH, 6 AS A STARTER

# PLAIN AND HERB DUMPLINGS FOR SOUPS AND STEWS

These are the old-fashioned suet dumplings, once commonly served with beef stew, and a stalwart of British cooking for generations. Wonderful filling stodge for a cold day, and far too nice to leave to the carnivores.

110 g (4 oz) self-raising flour
  (or use plain flour and add 2 level teaspoons baking powder)
pinch of salt
60 g (2 oz) vegetarian suet
cold water to mix

Sift the flour and salt into a large bowl. Mix in the suet. Using a round-ended knife, gradually stir in cold water until the mixture starts to cohere. Be careful not to add too much.

Finish bringing the mixture together using your hand, and knead it lightly for a very short time, just until it sticks together in a manageable and not too sticky dough.

Divide it into 8–9 roughly equal portions and roll into balls, using your hands. A little extra flour may be necessary to prevent sticking.

Drop into the soup or stew for the last 25 minutes of cooking time, and simmer gently in a covered pan.

HERB DUMPLINGS

A couple of tablespoons of finely chopped fresh herbs can be added before the water is stirred in. Don't use too many herbs at once – one, or two at the most, is fine.

SERVES 2–3

# SALADS

*A well-constructed salad can be a meal in itself, and is one of the best and easiest ways of using fresh, home-grown produce. I often wander round the garden allowing ripeness to dictate the salad of the day – a treat when inspiration is otherwise lacking. This is particularly useful in the earliest stages of cropping when you don't have very much of any one thing. A few interesting leaves, some fresh herbs, radishes, perhaps a tomato or two, a handful of beans, and you have the makings of a meal. Pad it out with some roasted walnuts, cubes of Emmental cheese and some decent bread, and dinner begins to sound quite promising. Happily, most supermarkets now sell a good range of pre-packed mixed salad leaves, and interesting salads are no longer the sole preserve of gardeners.*

*Some of these salads are stand-alone, others are definitely accompaniments for more substantial dishes. Some are very seasonal in nature, others can be made all the year round.*

# GARDEN LEAF AND HERB SALAD WITH BALSAMIC VINAIGRETTE

This is one for the gardeners. It probably isn't practical unless you grow at least some of the ingredients yourself, however if you too get carried away by the salad sections of seed catalogues, here is something nice to do with the end results. This isn't a recipe to be followed strictly – more a list of suggestions. I have categorised a large number of ingredients into groups with common characteristics and it's nice, although not crucial, to try and include something from each group. The object is to have a good balance of leaves, with contrasting flavours, colours and textures, but the salad can be as simple or as complicated as time, ingredients and your inclinations allow.

GROUP A, MILD FLAVOURS,
ESSENTIAL, USE 3 OR 4 GENEROUSLY
Little Gem lettuce
Iceberg lettuce
red frilly lettuce, such as Lollo Rossa
red oak leaf lettuce
green oak leaf lettuce
Cos lettuce
any other fancy lettuce you can find

GROUP B, STRONG FLAVOURS,
OPTIONAL, USE 1 OR 2 WITH RESTRAINT
red mustard leaves
Indian mustard leaves
mizuna
rocket
mibuna
sorrel
wild garlic leaves

GROUP C, SWEET AND MILD,
OPTIONAL, USE AS MANY
AS YOU CAN GET, IN MODERATION
baby spinach leaves
baby rainbow chard leaves
claytonia, also known as purslane
pea shoots
sprouted seeds

FRESH CHOPPED HERB LEAVES,
ESSENTIAL, USE 1 OR 2
mint
coriander
chervil
tarragon
basil
lovage (sparingly)
chives
Welsh onion tops, finely sliced
spring onion tops, finely sliced

EDIBLE FLOWERS,
OPTIONAL BUT PRETTY,
USE WITH RESTRAINT TO GARNISH
nasturtiums
borage
chive flowers
pot marigold petals
    (Calendula, not Tagetes)
violets (Viola *odorata* only)
rose petals

VINAIGRETTE DRESSING
2 tablespoons olive oil
1½ tablespoons balsamic vinegar
salt and freshly ground black pepper

Group A provides the bulk – mild in flavour and a good vehicle for the herbs and dressing. Use as many of these as you want and have available – try to ensure you have a mixture of green and red leaves, both soft and crunchy.

Group B contains some strongly-flavoured leaves, which will be very noticeable in the salad. Most of them are only obtainable as seed, but are easy to grow. Use them sparingly, and if they are large, tear or cut them into smaller pieces. Even one item from this group will lift your salad out of the ordinary. These are flavours that people will either love or hate, so until you know what the reaction will be, use them in moderation. I would be unlikely to use more than two items from this group in one salad.

Group C comprises some less common saladings, sweet and mild in flavour, which I have included for novelty value. Pea shoots are a great delicacy, but if you want to try them you'll probably have to grow them yourself, as I've never seen them for sale. They're very easy to grow. Buy a packet of culinary pea seeds, sow them in compost in a pot or seed tray, water, and keep in a light place. When they germinate snip off the top 5 cm (2 inches) with scissors when the little plants are about 10 cm (4 inches) tall. They should re-sprout a couple of times, enabling you to get more than one cut.

Wash the leaves selected from groups A, B and C, and dry them scrupulously with a salad spinner or tea towel. Cut or tear them into pieces of a suitable size and place in a large salad bowl. Wash the selected herbs, dry them, chop coarsely and add to the salad.

If you are using flowers, satisfy yourself that they've not been sprayed (or peed on by animals) as it is not really feasible to wash them. Only use flowers you know you can identify correctly – many flowers are poisonous. Gather them on a dry day, inspect carefully for wildlife, and remove all parts except the petals. You can store them in a sealed box or bag in the bottom of the fridge for a couple of hours, but they are best picked immediately prior to use.

Mix the vinaigrette ingredients by shaking them together in a screw-top jar. Just before serving, dress the salad and toss. Use enough dressing so that all the leaves are lightly coated, but not so much that you're left with a pool in the bottom of the bowl. Scatter the flower petals on top of the salad.

# ARTICHOKE, EGG AND TOMATO SALAD WITH PESTO MARINADE

A can or bottle of artichoke hearts in brine is a useful thing to have in your cupboard. When preserved in this way they need a bit more jazzing up than if fresh, but are considerably less hassle to prepare! I suggest you avoid the type that are sold in a liquid containing vinegar, as the flavour is all-pervasive, nasty and impossible to eradicate. This salad is substantial enough to make a meal in itself, accompanied by a chunk or two of decent bread.

THE SALAD

**about 400 g (14 oz) canned or bottled artichoke hearts in brine**
**2 eggs**
**12 or more Kalamata or other large black olives**
**a crisp lettuce: Cos, Iceberg or similar – leaves washed, dried and torn into pieces**
**12 or more ripe cherry tomatoes cut in half**

THE PESTO MARINADE

**2 heaped teaspoons of pesto, bought or home-made (recipe on page 191)**
**2 tablespoons Champagne vinegar**
**2 tablespoons olive oil**
**salt and freshly ground black pepper**

Drain and rinse the artichoke hearts in cold water, then dry them on kitchen paper.

Make the marinade by combining all the ingredients in a screw-top jar and shaking it.

Cut the artichoke hearts into quarters, then put them in your salad bowl, pour over the marinade, and leave them to soak up the flavour for at least 2 hours.

Meanwhile boil the eggs for 8–10 minutes, then drain and put them to cool in cold water (this prevents a green line from forming around the yolk).

When you're ready to serve the salad, shell and quarter the eggs. If you feel like making a special effort then pre-stone the olives, but I generally don't bother.

Put all the ingredients except the eggs into the bowl with the artichoke hearts, and toss thoroughly so everything is well-coated with marinade. Arrange the egg chunks on top and serve immediately.

SERVES 2 AS A MAIN COURSE, 4 AS A SIDE SALAD

# WATERCRESS, AVOCADO AND WALNUT SALAD

A useful salad which can be made virtually all the year round, this has some nice contrasts of texture and flavour. It is substantial enough to make a starter or even a light lunch if served with some decent bread.

THE SALAD
**bunch of watercress, washed, trimmed and dried**
**$\frac{1}{2}$ a small Iceberg lettuce, the outer leaves discarded, inner leaves torn up**
**10 or 12 ripe cherry tomatoes, washed, dried and halved**
**1 large ripe avocado**
**small handful of roasted, chopped walnuts (see page 16 for roasting times)**

THE DRESSING
**2 tablespoons olive oil**
**$1\frac{1}{2}$ tablespoons balsamic vinegar**
**salt and freshly ground black pepper**

Put the watercress, iceberg lettuce, and tomatoes in a salad bowl.

Make the dressing by shaking the ingredients together in a screw-top jar.

Peel and dice the avocado. If it is reluctant to shed its skin the following method may help. Cut the avocado in half and remove the stone. Lay the avocado half skin-side down on a chopping board and, using a sharp knife, gently score through the flesh in a grid pattern, without cutting through the skin. Now push the skin from behind, turning it inside out, so the chunks separate. They can then be detached quite easily using a spoon.

Add the avocado chunks to the salad, and toss it all together with the oil and vinegar dressing. Scatter the roasted walnuts over the salad and serve immediately.

SERVES 2 AS A STARTER, 4 AS A SIDE SALAD

# SUMMER BEAN SALAD

Mainly because I prefer them that way, but partly from laziness, I like to pick beans from the garden when they are still small enough to require no preparation other than 'top and tailing'. At about 10 cm (4 inches) long and less than pencil thickness, they are tender and delicate, requiring only minimal cooking. If, as invariably happens, you end up with beans of greatly differing size, it is worth grading them into two or three batches to be cooked separately, the largest for a couple of minutes longer than the smaller ones.

230 g (8 oz) baby runner beans
230 g (8 oz) baby golden French beans
1 tablespoon olive oil
1 tablespoon Champagne vinegar
salt and freshly ground black pepper
1 teaspoon chopped tarragon
1 tablespoon chopped chives

Wash, top and tail both types of beans, keeping them separate. Boil or steam them in separate batches, until just tender but still with some bite. For very small, tender beans this can take as little as 3 minutes, but larger, tougher beans may take 10 minutes or more – you'll need to keep testing them. For the pros and cons of steaming versus boiling see page 16.

Make a dressing by mixing the oil and vinegar in a large bowl with a little salt and pepper. As soon as each batch of beans is cooked, put them into the bowl with the dressing. They seem to absorb the flavouring better if marinaded while they are still warm. Don't add the herbs until just before serving, as they discolour.

The beans can be served warm or cold.

SERVES 2–3

# YELLOW COURGETTE AND ROCKET SALAD

This lovely zingy salad makes a good accompaniment to pasta or other stodge. The mustard leaves are by no means essential, but will add an extra dimension if you can find them. Giant red mustard is very fast and easy to grow from seed, especially during spring or autumn. It can suffer quite badly from flea beetle damage during the summer.

230 g (8 oz) small yellow courgettes, no more than finger thickness
110 g (4 oz) rocket leaves
2 large or several small leaves of giant red mustard
1 tablespoon olive oil
juice of half a lemon
salt and freshly ground black pepper

Wash and dry the courgettes, rocket and mustard leaves. Slice the courgettes thinly, cutting them on the diagonal. If the rocket leaves are quite large, cut them into 2 or 3 pieces. Cut the mustard leaves into fine shreds. Toss the leaves and courgettes together, then add the olive oil, salt and pepper, and toss again, until the leaves are evenly coated. Finally, toss in the lemon juice and serve immediately.

SERVES 2–3

# WARM FLAGEOLET SALAD WITH FRESH HERBS

This is a nice winter salad, for those occasions when you fancy something with the tang of vinaigrette but recoil from the idea of anything chilly.

THE BEANS

120 g (4½ oz) dried flageolet beans, soaked in water overnight,
    or a 400 g (13 oz) tin of cooked flageolet beans, rinsed and drained

THE DRESSING

1 spring onion, finely chopped
1 tablespoon olive oil
1 tablespoon of Champagne vinegar
1 pinch of sugar
2 teaspoons of lemon juice
salt and freshly ground black pepper

TO SERVE

2 tablespoons fresh mint, chopped
2 tablespoons fresh tarragon, chopped

If using dried beans, rinse the soaked beans thoroughly under copious running water. Place in a pan with fresh water, bring to the boil and simmer gently until they are tender. The time this takes will depend on the condition and age of the beans, and can be up to 2 hours. Test them from time to time, starting after about 1 hour. If using tinned beans, give them a good rinse, then put them in a pan with a little water and heat them gently.

In a small bowl, mix together all the dressing ingredients. When the beans are cooked (or hot) drain them thoroughly, return them to the pan in which they were cooked, and pour on the dressing while the beans are still hot. Stir, so they are evenly coated, and allow them to cool for a couple of minutes.

Immediately before serving, stir in the freshly chopped green herbs. If you add them too soon, they will lose their brightness.

SERVES 2

# PINK GRAPEFRUIT AND WATERCRESS SALAD

This salad is fruity and astringent – just the thing for a dull winter day when you feel in need of something enlivening. It makes an excellent companion dish for carbohydrate comfort food such as *Couscous with saffron and butter beans* (page 87).

1 pink grapefruit
2 Little Gem lettuce or 1 small Iceberg
large bunch of watercress, trimmed
2 tablespoons olive oil
a few roasted walnut pieces (see page 16 for roasting times)
1 tablespoon balsamic vinegar
salt and freshly ground black pepper

Using the sharpest knife you possess, peel the grapefruit, removing peel, pith and the thin skin from the outside surface of the fruit, all in one go. A gentle sawing movement is what's needed. Now hold the grapefruit over a bowl to catch the juice, and carefully remove each segment from its skin by slicing either side of it towards the centre of the fruit. Put the naked grapefruit segments in the bowl with the juice, and when you've finished, squeeze the remains hard in your hand over the bowl to extract the juice.

Wash and dry the lettuce and watercress and put them in the salad bowl. Dress with the olive oil, making sure the leaves are evenly coated. Add the grapefruit and its juice, the walnuts and balsamic vinegar, toss the salad, season with a little salt and pepper and toss again. Serve immediately.

SERVES 2

# GUACAMOLE

Hardly original, but this is a nice version of the classic, and useful to include in a Mexican meal. Make this as near to serving as possible – it goes brown if kept sitting around.

½ a small red onion, very finely chopped
½ to 1 fresh or frozen red chilli (depending on strength),
    de-seeded and finely chopped
a handful of fresh coriander leaves, washed, dried and chopped
juice from ½ a lime
2 large ripe avocados or 3 small ones
salt and freshly ground black pepper

Prepare the onion, chilli, coriander and lime juice before you deal with the avocados. As always, I recommend wearing rubber gloves when handling fresh chillies. Cut the avocados in half and scoop out the flesh with a spoon. Mash it with a fork, so as to retain some texture, then stir in the other ingredients and check the seasoning. You may need to add more lime juice too.

SERVES 3 ON TOAST FOR LUNCH, MORE AS PART OF A MEXICAN MEAL

# PASTA SALAD WITH GREEN BEANS AND TOMATOES

This salad is quite substantial enough to provide dinner for two, and makes for good hot-weather eating.

2 tablespoons olive oil
2 tablespoons balsamic vinegar
3 rounded teaspoons pesto sauce, bought or home-made (recipe on page 191)
150 g (5 oz) pasta spirals, cooked in boiling water until *al dente*
200 g (7 oz) baby runner beans or French beans,
   cut into 4 cm (2 inch) lengths and steamed until *al dente*
1 large or 2 small shallots, peeled and very finely chopped
250 g (9 oz) cherry or other well-flavoured tomatoes, cut into chunks
about 12 fresh basil leaves, shredded
salt and freshly ground black pepper

Make a vinaigrette by mixing the olive oil, balsamic vinegar and pesto. Ready-prepared pesto of the type available everywhere in jars is quite acceptable here. Cook and drain the pasta and beans (separately), and while both are still warm stir in the vinaigrette and shallots. Allow the salad to cool for at least 5 minutes before adding the tomatoes and basil. Season to taste with salt and pepper. This salad is equally good either chilled or lukewarm.

SERVES 2 FOR DINNER, 4 AS AN ACCOMPANIMENT

# PINK BEETROOT SALAD WITH ROASTED WALNUTS AND WALNUT VINAIGRETTE

I make this salad with home-grown pink beetroot *Barabietola di Chioggia*, pulled at ping-pong ball size or smaller. It is very straightforward to grow, provided your soil is not too heavy, and looks utterly delectable on the plate, like little glistening rose buds. It has a more delicate flavour than the ordinary dark purple beets, but if these are all you can get they'll be fine – the dish will be more robust, that's all. For any beetroot virgins out there, be warned – the purple type stains absolutely everything including your urine! I've known people be quite alarmed by this harmless side effect.

350 g (12 oz) uncooked baby beetroot, preferably pink
1 tablespoon walnut oil
1 tablespoon balsamic vinegar
salt and freshly ground black pepper
1 tablespoon snipped fresh chives or Welsh onion greens
2 tablespoons chopped roasted walnuts (see page 16 for roasting times)

Twist off the leaves from the beetroots, leaving an inch or so of stalk attached. Don't trim the roots, or you'll make the beetroots bleed.  Gently wash off any adhering soil, using a soft brush. Simmer the beetroots in a covered pan of water until they are tender.  The time this takes will depend on the age, size and toughness of the beetroots, and can vary considerably.  Start testing (press with the back of a fork – there should be a slight give) after 30 minutes and be prepared to go on cooking them for up to $1\frac{1}{2}$ hours. If they're not tender after $1\frac{1}{2}$ hours, they never will be!

When you think they are done, drain them and leave until they are cool enough to handle.  Top and tail them and rub off the skins using your fingers.  Pink beetroot doesn't stain but the purple varieties do, so if you care about these things, wear rubber gloves. Slice the beetroot into wedges or just halves, depending on the size, then dress with the oil and vinegar.  This much can be done a few hours ahead of time.  Season to taste with salt and pepper, and just before serving sprinkle on the herbs and walnuts.

SERVES 2–3 AS A SIDE DISH

# POTATO SALAD WITH CHIVES AND CRÈME FRAÎCHE

This is a very simple and very delicious potato salad. Like all very simple recipes the outcome depends almost entirely on the quality of the ingredients, so get the best potatoes you can find. If you grow or can buy unusual salad varieties such as *Pink Fir Apple* or *Ratte* this is a lovely way to serve them.

450 g (1 lb) small salad potatoes, washed but not peeled, and left whole
3 spring onions, thinly sliced, including some green,
   or 1 shallot, peeled and very finely chopped
100 g (3½ oz) crème fraîche
salt and freshly ground black pepper
about 15 g (½ oz) fresh chives or other herbs (see variations below)

Steam or boil the potatoes in salted water until tender but not disintegrating. The choice of cooking method really depends on the potato variety – some tend to fall apart if boiled, so steam if you're not sure how a particular spud will behave.

Stir the spring onions or shallots into the crème fraîche, and add the hot, drained potatoes. Stir very gently to coat them, season with salt and pepper to taste, then allow the salad to cool.

Add the clean, dry, sliced chives just before serving. Although it is usually served cold, I like this salad when it's still slightly warm – it certainly shouldn't be chilled.

SERVES 2–3

HERB VARIATIONS

Substitute another green herb (tarragon, mint, basil, lovage, dill, etc.) for the chives, depending on what you're serving with the salad. For instance, use shredded basil and serve the salad with *Terrine of green and yellow beans with tomato* (page 66).

# POTATO SALAD WITH A PARSLEY LEMON DRESSING

This is really just a variation on the preceding recipe, although the lemon makes it quite distinctive. The ratio of crème fraîche to yogurt can be varied, although I would be disinclined to use all yogurt.

450 g (1 lb) small salad potatoes, washed but not peeled, and left whole
60 g (2 oz) crème fraîche
60 g (2 oz) plain yogurt
about 15 g (½ oz) fresh parsley, finely chopped
2 teaspoons of very finely chopped red onion
2 teaspoons grated rind from a well scrubbed lemon
salt and freshly ground black pepper

Cook the potatoes as described in the previous recipe.

Mix together all the remaining ingredients, and pour over the potatoes while they're still hot. Allow to cool slightly before serving. As with the previous potato salad, I prefer this slightly warm or at room temperature, but not chilled.

SERVES 2–3

# WARM LENTIL AND MINT SALAD

This salad is made with the small, green, French Puy lentils, which are now quite easy to find in supermarkets and delis. They hold their shape and colour better than most other lentils, having less of a tendency to disintegrate into sludge. As with all beans and pulses, they should only be salted after they are cooked – if you salt the cooking water they may stay obstinately tough.

170 g (6 oz) Puy lentils
2 tablespoons olive oil
2 tablespoons Champagne vinegar
2 heaped tablespoons chopped fresh mint
½ level teaspoon salt
3 or 4 spring onions, sliced, including some green
110 g (4 oz) cherry tomatoes, quartered

Rinse the lentils in a sieve with plenty of cold running water and pick out any stones.

Simmer them in unsalted water for about 25–30 minutes, until tender but still with some bite.

Drain them, put them back in the pan and immediately mix in the oil, vinegar, mint and salt. Allow the lentils to cool slightly, stirring occasionally so they are evenly coated in the dressing.

Carefully mix in the tomatoes and spring onions just before serving.

Don't be tempted to leave the tomatoes whole, no matter how small they are. Part of the appeal of this dish is the way some of their juice runs, combining with the dressing.

SERVES 2 FOR LUNCH, 4 AS A SIDE DISH

VARIATION – WARM LENTIL AND AVOCADO SALAD

Stir in a perfectly ripe, diced avocado and a little lemon juice just before serving.

VARIATION – MINTED LENTIL SALAD WITH FETA

Slice a little feta cheese over each portion and drizzle with green olive oil just before serving. Place a few finely-sliced ribbons of fresh mint on top of the cheese, where they will look pretty, the green against the white.

# MAIN COURSES

*From everyday quick meals to sophisticated dinner party dishes, you'll find a wide selection here. I like to eat according to the season and where appropriate I make recommendations about what time of year a dish is best served. Some foods are just more suited to certain times of year than others, and many vegetables have a definite peak when they are at their best.*

# SOUFFLÉ OF CHARD AND TOMATO

A soufflé is impressive. There is something fundamentally intriguing about food which transforms itself so dramatically. Into the oven it goes – a pool of runny custard in the bottom of a dish, and a short time later out it comes, puffed up into a fragrant, golden, gravity-defying dome.

Despite the magic, soufflés are really very straightforward to make provided you adhere to a couple of basic principles. Firstly, in order to whisk egg whites successfully both whisk and bowl must be scrupulously clean and dry. Even a speck of oil or moisture will prevent them fluffing up. Secondly, a cooked soufflé waits for no-one so make sure the diners are seated and ready before you carry it swiftly from oven to table. Almost as soon as it leaves the oven a soufflé will start to deflate as the air inside it cools.

TO COOK THE CHARD
**230 g (8 oz) Swiss chard leaves**
**15 g (½ oz) butter**
**1 tablespoon olive oil**
**2 cloves garlic, crushed**

FOR THE SAUCE
**15 g (½ oz) butter**
**1 rounded tablespoon plain white flour**
**180 ml (6½ fl oz) milk**

TO FINISH THE SOUFFLÉ
**170 g (6 oz) grated mature Cheddar cheese**
**60 g (2 oz) sun-dried tomato paste**
**salt and freshly ground black pepper to taste**
**4 eggs, separated**
**cream of tartar (optional)**

Oven temperature: 190°C (375°F, gas 5) – adjust for fan ovens

Cut out and discard the thick ribs of the chard, but don't throw them away – they're delicious. You can use them in another recipe, or just steam them separately as a vegetable accompaniment for the soufflé. Slice the chard leaves into narrow ribbons, wash them thoroughly and drain well. Spin them if you have a salad spinner, otherwise pat dry with a tea towel.

Heat the oil and butter in a wide frying pan and sauté the chard leaves uncovered, over a moderate heat, until tender and dry-ish. How long this takes will depend on the size and age of the chard. Add the crushed garlic towards the end of the cooking time, then set aside.

In a medium-sized saucepan make a roux sauce using the butter, flour and milk. If you need help with the method, follow the detailed instructions on page 184.

Take the pan off the heat, then stir in the cheese. When the cheese has melted and the sauce is smooth, stir in the tomato paste and season with salt and freshly ground black pepper. Allow the sauce to cool slightly – if your pan is very heavy and heat-retentive, plunge its base into cold water for a minute or two to avoid scrambling the egg yolks – then beat in the egg yolks, one by one. Stir the cooked chard leaves into the sauce.

Pre-heat the oven now if you haven't already done so.

In a large bowl, whisk the egg whites using an electric mixer (or a wire balloon whisk) until they form stiff, snowy peaks. For this to work, both bowl and beaters must be scrupulously dry. If you have any cream of tartar, add a pinch while whisking, as it will make the soufflé lighter, but it's not crucial.

Stir a heaped tablespoon or two of egg white into the sauce to slacken it, then push the egg whites to one side in their mixing bowl. Carefully tip the sauce in the other side (to avoid deflating the egg whites) and gently fold the mixture together using a large metal spoon. If a few small fragments of egg white remain visible this is fine, and probably better than over-zealous mixing, the aim being to retain air.

Tip the mixture into a buttered 15–20 cm (6–8 inch) soufflé dish and bake in the oven for 25–30 minutes until well-risen and golden brown on top. You can tell if the soufflé is cooked by sticking in a metal skewer through its side. If it comes out clean you won't have a runny middle; however, I consider a slightly runny middle to be desirable. It's entirely subjective.

Serve immediately, before the soufflé sinks.

SERVES 2–3

# SOUFFLÉ OF SMALL PUMPKINS, BAKED IN THEIR SKINS

These individual soufflés look very appealing, baked in their own skins, and would make a nice centrepiece to an autumn dinner party. Choose pumpkin varieties such as *Jack be Little* or *Munchkins*, which will sit without wobbling.

3 larger or 6 small mini pumpkins
salt and freshly ground black pepper
30 g (1 oz) butter, plus a little extra for roasting the pumpkins
2 level tablespoons plain flour
150 ml (5 fl oz) milk, perhaps a little more
170 g (6 oz) grated Gruyere cheese
4 large eggs
4 tablespoons chopped fresh chives

Oven temperature: 180°C (350°F, gas 4) – adjust for fan ovens

Using a small sharp knife, cut out lids from the tops of the pumpkins. Discard the lids. Scoop out all the seeds and fibrous matter using a teaspoon or melon-baller. Season the inside of each pumpkin with a little salt and pepper, and put a small piece of butter in each one. Butter or oil a baking tray, and arrange the pumpkins on it so they are not touching each other. Bake uncovered in the pre-heated oven for 30–50 minutes, until the pumpkins are cooked. The time depends on both size and variety, so test the flesh for softness with a knife point (on the inside – don't pierce the skins).

When cooked, set the pumpkins on one side until they are cool enough to handle. Scoop the flesh out of the skins carefully. Leave a thin layer of pumpkin flesh attached, to improve their rigidity, since they are to be used as containers. Mash the flesh coarsely with a fork or potato masher.

Increase the oven temperature to 200°C (400°F, gas 6) – adjust for fan ovens.

Make a roux sauce using the butter, flour and milk. If you're not sure how to do it, follow the detailed instructions on page 184. When the sauce has thickened, remove the pan from the heat and stir in the pumpkin purée, grated cheese and egg yolks. Season with salt and pepper. If the mixture is really unmanageably thick, add a little extra milk, but it should be quite thick, and take some physical effort to stir.

In a large bowl, whisk the egg whites until they stand up in stiff snowy peaks. Both bowl and whisk must be scrupulously dry. Stir a spoonful of egg white into the pumpkin mixture just to slacken it slightly then, using a metal spoon, gently fold the pumpkin mixture into the egg whites. Fold in the chopped chives, then spoon the mixture into the pumpkin shells. There may be some mixture left over, in which case spoon it into a small, buttered soufflé dish and cook with the others.

Bake for 15–20 minutes, until well risen and golden brown on top. You can stick a thin sharp knife into the side of the soufflé to check the internal consistency if you don't like them too runny. Serve speedily, before they deflate.

SERVES 3

# SORREL SOUFFLÉ

Another one for the gardeners since you're unlikely to find sorrel in the shops in sufficient quantity to make this dish. If you have a little garden space in which to grow a few vegetables, sorrel is simple, quick and trouble-free in cultivation, and with its lemony tang, makes a useful addition to salads, as well as a wonderful ingredient for sauces, soups and soufflés, as here. Although perennial, it is best re-grown from seed every year as it coarsens with age.

1 washing-up bowl of fresh sorrel leaves – the exact quantity is unimportant
60 g (2 oz) butter
60 g (2 oz) flour
280 ml (10 fl oz) milk
110 g (4 oz) freshly grated Parmesan cheese
salt and freshly ground black pepper
6 eggs, separated
cream of tartar (optional)

Oven temperature: 190°C (375°F, gas 5) – adjust for fan ovens

Wash the sorrel thoroughly. Spin it in a salad spinner, or dry it in a clean tea towel, then cram it into a large pan (no need to add water), and wilt it over a moderate heat. Turn the leaves over and over, much as you might toss a salad, so they cook evenly. They will virtually disappear, the mountain of raw leaves turning into a few spoonfuls of intense green slush. Set aside while you make the sauce which forms the basis of the soufflé.

Pre-heat the oven if you haven't already done so.

Make a roux sauce using the butter, flour and milk, following the detailed instructions on page 184 if you need help with the method.

When all the milk has been added to the sauce, stir in the drained, wilted sorrel. Take the pan off the heat, stir in about three quarters of the cheese (save the rest for the top), and season with salt and freshly ground black pepper. Allow the sauce to cool slightly, then beat in the egg yolks, one by one.

In a large bowl, whisk the egg whites using an electric mixer (or a wire balloon whisk) until they form stiff, snowy peaks. Both bowl and beaters must be scrupulously dry. Add a pinch of cream of tartar (if you have any) while whisking – it makes the soufflé lighter.

Stir a heaped tablespoon of egg white into the sauce to slacken it, then push the egg whites to one side in their mixing bowl, carefully tip the sauce in the other side and gently fold the mixture together using a metal spoon. The idea is to amalgamate the two, with minimum loss of air. If a few small fragments of egg white remain distinct, this is fine, and probably better than over-mixing.

Tip the mixture into a buttered 20 cm (8 inch) soufflé dish, sprinkle over the remaining cheese and bake in the oven for 25–30 minutes until well-risen and golden brown on top. Serve immediately.

SERVES 4

# TERRINE OF GREEN AND YELLOW BEANS WITH TOMATO

When sliced, this terrine looks quite striking, with its polka-dot cross-sections of green and yellow beans in a pink tomato-flavoured matrix. It can be served as a starter with *Tomato coulis* (page 192), but if accompanied by *Potato salad with chives and crème fraîche* (page 57) and some crisp green leaves, it is substantial enough for a main course. Remember to allow for a little cooling time, as the terrine is best served lukewarm.

230 g (8 oz) French beans, preferably a yellow variety
230 g (8 oz) runner beans
a small amount of butter, for oiling the terrine
4 eggs
3 tablespoons full fat creamy Greek yogurt or double cream
60 g (2 oz) fresh Parmesan cheese, finely grated
4 heaped teaspoons concentrated tomato purée
salt and freshly ground black pepper

Oven temperature: 180°C (350°F, gas 4) – adjust for fan ovens

Wash, top and tail the beans and, keeping the two types separate, boil them in plenty of salted water in uncovered pans until they are just cooked, but still retain a little bite. This will probably take 3–8 minutes, depending on the condition of the beans. As soon as they are done drain them swiftly, rinse them briefly in cold water and dry with kitchen towels. This method of cooking preserves the colour, which is important for this recipe.

Butter the inside of a 450 g (1 lb) loaf tin (or deep rectangular ceramic terrine of similar size). Line the base and long sides with a single piece of grease-proof or silicon paper.

Pre-heat the oven, if you if you haven't already done so.

Mix both types of beans together and arrange them lengthwise in the tin so they are evenly distributed in more or less parallel lines. You're aiming for a neat, two-tone, polka-dot effect when the terrine is sliced.

Beat the eggs, and stir in the cream or yogurt, Parmesan and tomato purée. Season with salt and pepper. Pour the egg mixture carefully over the beans, making sure all the beans are submerged – poke them down if necessary. Set the tin in a deep tray containing 10 cm (2 inches) of boiling water and bake for about 30 minutes until set.

Allow the terrine to cool in the tin for two or three minutes, before turning it out onto a flat dish. Leave to cool until just lukewarm, allowing the flavour to intensify.

Cut into 2 cm (1 inch) slices and serve each slice on a little pool of *Tomato coulis* (page 192).

SERVES 4 FOR DINNER, 6 AS A STARTER

# COURGETTE AND POTATO FRITTATA

Frittata, really just a hefty omelette – like a quiche without the pastry – is a versatile dish. Straight from the pan and served with salad and bread, it makes a good and speedy hot dinner. It can also be cooled to room temperature and cut into wedges, in which state it is quite portable, for a lunch box or picnic.

230 g (8 oz) small well-flavoured potatoes, such as Pink Fir Apple
230 g (8 oz) courgettes
15 g (½ oz) butter
1 tablespoon olive oil
4–5 large eggs
2 tablespoons fresh Parmesan cheese, finely grated
2 tablespoons finely chopped parsley or basil
salt and freshly ground black pepper

Scrub the potatoes and simmer in salted water until just tender, but still with some bite. Drain and cool them and, when cool enough to handle, slice into 5 mm (¼ inch) rounds. With small salad potatoes there's really no need to peel them. Leave them on one side while you cook the courgettes.

Wash and cut the courgettes into 5 mm (¼ inch) slices, then sauté them over a moderate heat in a 25 cm (10 inch) frying pan, in the butter and oil, until about two thirds cooked. This may only take a couple of minutes, depending on the age and size of the courgettes.

Meanwhile beat the eggs in a large bowl, just enough to combine them, and stir in the Parmesan cheese, parsley or basil, salt and pepper. Add the potatoes and courgettes to the egg mixture. Scrape any debris from the frying pan, add a small amount of olive oil if the pan seems completely dry, and pour the egg mixture into the pan.

Cook without stirring and with the pan uncovered, over a low heat until the bottom of the frittata is set. This should take about 10 minutes, but check the centre before attempting to turn it. Loosen the edges and slide a thin spatula under the frittata to help it on its way. Give the pan a shake to make sure the frittata is detached before attempting to turn it. Invert a dinner plate over the frying pan, then, holding pan and dinner plate as one, turn everything upside down and tip the frittata onto the plate. Slide it back into the pan on its uncooked side, and give it a few more minutes to finish cooking.

If the business with the dinner plate sounds too daunting, the frittata can be finished under a hot grill. Serve hot or just lukewarm, as you prefer. The flavours emerge more strongly at the lower temperature, but don't serve it chilled.

SERVES 2 OR 3 AS A MAIN COURSE

# PUMPKIN AND SWEETCORN FRITTATA

This cheerful, golden frittata is like a ripe harvest in the pan. Excellent made in the autumn with fresh corn and the first of the pumpkin crop, it is almost as good later in the year, made from stored pumpkin and frozen corn.

1 pumpkin (or a slice of one) weighing around 270 g (9 oz)
4 eggs
3 tablespoons chopped fresh chives
½ a Habanero or other hot chilli, finely chopped
salt and freshly ground black pepper
2 cobs of corn or 170 g (6 oz) frozen sweetcorn kernels
15 g (½ oz) butter
1 tablespoon olive oil
1 medium onion, chopped
1 clove of garlic, chopped
110 g (4 oz) feta cheese, crumbled

First cook the pumpkin. Halve, peel and de-seed it and then steam the chunks until tender (anything between 5 and 20 minutes – they vary a lot!). If you have the oven on for something else you can bake it cut side down in the oven until tender. When it's cool enough to handle, scoop the flesh away from the skin and mash it coarsely with a fork or potato masher (leave a few lumps).

Whisk the eggs with a fork, just enough to amalgamate them, and whisk in the mashed pumpkin, chives, chilli, salt and pepper.

If using fresh corn, strip the kernels off the cobs using a small, sharp knife.

Heat the butter and oil in a 25 cm (10 inch) frying pan, then fry the onion over a moderate heat until quite soft (about 10–15 minutes). Add the un-cooked sweetcorn and garlic and fry. Don't cook it for long at this point, only a couple of minutes, as the corn should retain a bit of crunch. Spread the vegetables evenly in the pan, pour in the egg mixture, turn the heat down a little, and leave the frittata alone for 5–10 minutes, until the base is set but the top is still quite moist-looking. During this time pre-heat the grill.

Crumble the feta cheese over the frittata and put the frying pan under the grill, as close as possible to the heat source, for a few minutes until the cheese is brown and bubbling and the egg set.

Serve hot or (even better) at room temperature, with some decent bread and a crunchy green salad.

SERVES 2 AS A MAIN COURSE, 6 AS A STARTER

# LIFE WITHOUT PASTA?

How did we ever survive without pasta? It now seems unbelievable that dried spaghetti was once considered exotic and was virtually unobtainable outside of big cities, but for years now pasta has replaced potatoes as the staple stodge in our house. I simply could not conceive of life without it. It can be as fast or slow as you like – anything from fuel for the desperate, ready in under ten minutes, to the most sophisticated dinner-party dish imaginable.

Although fresh pasta is widely available I make no apologies for including recipes for it here. When made at home it is quite cosmically delicious and impresses the hell out of people; moreover, it's fun to make. You can customize the pasta according to the sauce you serve it with; you can vary the flour, by substituting part buckwheat or wholewheat; you can add fresh herbs, garlic or spinach, saffron or other aromatics. Although I recommend Italian pasta flour for the sake of authenticity, I have had very good results using ordinary plain white flour – the type used for cakes. With a little practice pasta can be made very quickly.

Most of the recipes that follow can be made with fresh or dry pasta as you see fit, but some require a specific type of fresh pasta. Pasta dough can be made ahead of time if necessary. Just wrap it in cling film and keep it in the fridge, for anything up to three days. It also freezes well.

Pasta is difficult to make without a machine. It needs to be a uniform thickness to cook evenly, and this is hard to achieve by hand. The small metal pasta machines that clamp onto the edge of a table and work like an old-fashioned laundry mangle are relatively inexpensive and easy to find. They are perfectly adequate for occasional domestic use, and great fun to play with.

In addition to those that follow you will find a few more sauces suitable for pasta in the sauces chapter starting on page 184.

# FRESH EGG PASTA

340 g (12 oz) unbleached plain white flour (Italian pasta flour, if you can get it)
2 level teaspoons salt
2 large eggs
2 teaspoons olive oil
cold water

In a bowl, mix the salt into the flour. Beat the eggs and oil together lightly, just to amalgamate, make a well in the centre of the flour, pour the egg into it and stir with a round-ended knife. Using your finger tips as if making pastry, rub the egg into the flour until it is evenly distributed throughout. The mixture should look like fine crumbs. Don't be in too much of a hurry here – even distribution of the egg throughout the flour is vital. This initial mixing can be done very easily with a food processor.

Tip the mixture onto a clean work surface and start adding cold water in very small quantities, just a teaspoon or so at a time. Using your fingers, mix in the water and see if the dough will start to stick together. It should be very firm and rather on the dry side at this point.

Begin kneading. Gather the dough together with your hands and press down on it, using the full weight of your body (your work surface needs to be quite low for this to be feasible). Flatten the dough with your hand, fold it over roughly in half and press down again. Give the squashed dough about a quarter turn, fold in half, press down again with as much force as you can muster. That's all there is to it. If the dough seems to be sticking to the work surface just sprinkle a little flour on it, but it probably won't be necessary.

If after about 2–3 minutes it is still very crumbly, a tiny amount of extra water can be added. Knead for about 10 minutes altogether, by which time the dough will be silky smooth, firm and quite elastic. Place in a sealed plastic bag in the fridge and leave it there for at least 1 hour, several if more convenient.

Flatten the chilled dough using your hands, and set your pasta machine's roller to the widest setting. Roll the dough through the machine a couple of times, to make it more pliable. Gradually reduce the thickness of the roller setting and put the dough through the machine. As it gets longer and thinner it will be more manageable if cut into several pieces. When the desired thickness is achieved, it can be made into ravioli, lasagne, etc. or passed through the appropriate cutter rollers.

The pasta may need to be dried off slightly before cooking, to prevent it sticking together. Hang spaghetti or noodles up to dry for about 10 minutes. I use a folding laundry dryer with rigid arms, but I've seen special wooden spaghetti dryers in kitchen shops. Alternatively if you have enough space, leave it flat on a floured counter. After around 10–15 minutes it should be dry enough to put in a plastic bag and refrigerate until you're ready to cook it. At this stage it can also be frozen.

The cooking is simplicity itself, and will take only about 1 minute, so make sure everything else is ready. Have plates or bowls warming, since pasta cools with astonishing rapidity. Also if you're serving a cream-based sauce, it will stay liquid for longer on a warm plate – a cold plate will make it congeal.

Bring a large pan of salted water to a rolling boil, then put in the pasta all in one go. Give it a swirl with a fork or spoon to separate the pieces. Have a colander waiting in the sink. You need to hover by the pan and test at regular intervals. As soon as the pasta is tender, which, depending on its precise thickness, can be as quickly as 30 seconds, whip it off the heat, drain in the colander, and serve.

MAKES ABOUT 600 G (21 OZ), ENOUGH FOR 4–6 SERVINGS

VARIATION: BUCKWHEAT PASTA

Replace one third of the pasta flour with buckwheat flour. You will need more water than usual, since buckwheat flour is very absorbent. In tests I used 3 tablespoons, but try mixing after 2, then add extra if necessary, to get a silky texture. The dough will be more crumbly and difficult to knead, but will come together with perseverance. It might be prudent to make the basic fresh pasta before attempting this variation, so you will know what the dough should feel like.

# HERB PASTA

Since pasta is usually boiled and herbs are volatile, much of the herb flavour goes down the plug hole with the cooking water. In the herb pasta variations given here I have allowed for this, and have included enough of the herb to give a subtle flavour to the pasta. If the pasta is intended for lasagne, or any other dish where it will be baked without pre-boiling, you may wish to reduce the amount of herbs slightly.

340 g (12 oz) unbleached plain white flour (Italian pasta flour if you can get it)
2 level teaspoons salt
2 large eggs
2 teaspoons olive oil
2 tablespoons of any herb from the following list:
    finely chopped parsley, basil, tarragon, chives, chervil
    or other mild-flavoured herb
or 1 tablespoon of any of the following more strongly-flavoured herbs:
    finely chopped garlic, rosemary, lovage or oregano
cold water to mix

Put the flour and salt in the food processor and whiz briefly to amalgamate them. Add the herbs, eggs and oil, and whiz again, so that the egg is evenly distributed throughout the flour. The mixture should look like fine crumbs.

Tip the mixture onto a clean work surface, make a well in the centre, and add cold water, a teaspoon at a time. Continue mixing and kneading as described in the detailed instructions for *Fresh egg pasta* (page opposite).

MAKES ABOUT 600 G (21 OZ), ENOUGH FOR 4–6 SERVINGS

# SPINACH PASTA

You can't really taste the spinach in this, but the pasta will be a beautiful fresh green. Select the accompanying sauce or filling, at least in part, for its complimentary colour.

340 g (12 oz) un-bleached plain white flour (Italian pasta flour, if you can get it)
2 level teaspoons salt
2 large eggs
2 teaspoons olive oil
60 g (2 oz) fresh young spinach leaves

Wash and dry the spinach leaves. Get the leaves as dry as possible, or your pasta may end up too moist.

Put the flour and salt in the food processor and whiz briefly to amalgamate them. Add the eggs and oil, and whiz again, so that the egg is evenly distributed throughout the flour. The mixture should look like fine crumbs.

Feed the spinach leaves a few at a time through the food processor chute with the motor running, then knead as for basic fresh pasta. You are unlikely to need any additional water, as the water content of the spinach should be enough to bind the dough. If anything you may have to knead in a little extra flour. If you don't have a food processor, purée the spinach by whatever means you have at your disposal and mix into the dough by hand, in place of water.

Tip the dough onto a clean work surface and continue mixing and kneading as described in the detailed instructions for *Fresh egg pasta* on page 70.

MAKES ABOUT 600 G (21 OZ), ENOUGH FOR 4–6 SERVINGS

# SAFFRON PASTA

Suffused with a golden glow, and flecked with the intense orange of saffron strands, this pasta looks quite delectable.

2 generous pinches of saffron threads
340 g (12 oz) un-bleached plain white flour (Italian pasta flour, if you can get it)
2 level teaspoons salt
2 large eggs
2 teaspoons olive oil

Soak the saffron threads in 4 tablespoons of boiling water, for at least 10 minutes.

Put the flour and salt in the food processor and whiz briefly to amalgamate them. Add the eggs and oil, and whiz again, so that the egg is evenly distributed throughout the flour. The mixture should look like fine crumbs.

Tip the mixture onto a clean work surface, make a well in the centre, and pour in the saffron and its soaking liquid. Continue mixing and kneading as described in the detailed instructions for *Fresh egg pasta* (page 70). You may need to add a small amount more water, depending on the flour used.

MAKES ABOUT 600 G (21 OZ), ENOUGH FOR 4–6 SERVINGS

# PASTA WITH MUSHROOMS, WALNUTS AND AVOCADO

Very quick, very easy and very nice – the whole thing can be ready in about twenty minutes flat. You need a fully-ripe avocado for this, as it must be soft enough to disintegrate slightly in the pan and lubricate the pasta.

a few chopped walnuts – a small handful is plenty for two
a little oil and butter for frying
110 g (4 oz) mushrooms, as fresh as possible, cleaned and sliced
150 g (5 oz) dry pasta spirals, or 250 g (9 oz) fresh
1 large ripe avocado
salt and freshly ground black pepper
fresh Parmesan cheese, grated

Warm a dry frying pan over a moderate heat and throw in the chopped walnuts. Keep stirring or shaking them until they start to colour and smell toasty, then tip them onto a plate. Put a little oil and butter in the still warm pan, and fry the mushrooms; meanwhile cook your pasta in plenty of boiling salted water. When both pasta and mushrooms are cooked, drain the pasta and add it to the mushroom pan, turning the heat down very low. Cut the avocado in half and scoop small teaspoonsful straight into the pan. Season to taste with salt and pepper, throw in the walnuts and some Parmesan cheese, stir well and serve on pre-warmed plates.

SERVES 2

VARIATION

A few ripe cherry tomatoes, cut in half, can be added at the end, for just long enough to heat though.

# PASTA WITH SAVOY CABBAGE, DOLCELATTE AND ROASTED WALNUTS

This is a lovely, robust winter dish, perfect for when you come in chilled from outside and need something a bit stodgy and warming. It is quite rich, so don't follow it with a heavy pudding.

15 g (½ oz) butter
1 tablespoon olive oil
1 small Savoy cabbage, finely shredded and washed
1 clove of garlic, crushed or finely chopped
salt and freshly ground black pepper
juice of half a lemon
2 teaspoons fennel seeds
150 g (5 oz) dry pasta spirals, or 250 g (9 oz) fresh
50g (2 oz) roasted walnut pieces (see page 16 for roasting times)
110 g (4 oz) Dolcelatte cheese, roughly cubed
2–3 tablespoons cream
fresh Parmesan, grated

Heat the butter and oil in a large pan, add the cabbage and garlic, a little salt, the lemon juice and the fennel seeds, stir and cover. Cook over a gentle heat, stirring occasionally until the cabbage is tender but still has some bite. This will take anything from 15–25 minutes. You shouldn't need to add extra water, but if it seems to be catching (which it might, if your pan is on the thin side), just add a tiny amount of hot water from the kettle.

Cook the pasta in plenty of salted water, timing it to be ready with the cabbage. When both are cooked, drain the pasta and put it in the pan with the cabbage. Keep the heat on low. Add the walnuts, Dolcelatte cheese, cream and a little grated Parmesan. Season with plenty of black pepper and extra salt if you think it needs it. Give it all a good stir and serve on warmed plates, just as the Dolcelatte starts to melt. Serve with extra Parmesan, a crisp green salad and chilled Frascati.

SERVES 2


VARIATION

Most types of cabbage work well in this dish. Even a kale, such as *Cavolo Nero*, would be good – the darker green making a nice contrast with the pale pasta and cheese. Some kales are rather tough and need de-stalking and a longer cooking time, so if in doubt, cook the kale before the pasta. It can be re-heated easily enough.

# FUSILLI WITH COURGETTES, BASIL AND PINE KERNELS

A late summer recipe, this looks best made with a mixture of small green and gold-skinned courgettes, but either alone is fine. If you're making it for a special meal use home-made *Pesto* (page 191), but if it's just for a quick bite then good quality commercial pesto is perfectly acceptable. *Fusilli* (pasta spirals) are a good vehicle for pesto (plenty of surface area for the sauce to stick to), and unlike noodles or spaghetti which clump together in an amorphous mass, they stay separate enough to mix in easily with the courgettes. The roasted pine kernels, added at the very last moment so they stay crisp, provide textural contrast.

15 g (½ oz) butter
1 tablespoon olive oil
500 g (1 lb) courgettes, sliced into 5mm (¼ inch) rounds
salt and freshly ground black pepper
150 g (5 oz) fusilli
about 90 g (3 oz) pesto sauce, home-made (page 191) or bought
2 tablespoons chopped fresh basil
50 g (2 oz) roasted pine kernels (see page 16 for roasting times)
fresh grated Parmesan cheese to serve
whole sprigs of fresh basil for garnishing

Heat the butter and oil in a large, heavy frying pan, and fry the courgettes briskly, stirring or shaking the pan from time to time. The idea is to brown them on the outside, while still retaining some bite. Add half a teaspoon of salt. The courgettes should take no more than 10 minutes to cook, much less if they're tiny, so put the pasta on to be ready at the same time. If the courgettes seem likely to be cooked before the pasta is ready just whip them off the heat for a few minutes. If the pesto sauce is very thick, dilute it with a tablespoon or two of pasta cooking water.

Throw the chopped basil leaves in with the courgettes for the final minute or two of cooking time, and add a few grinds of pepper. Thoroughly drain the pasta, which should be *al dente*, and tip it into the pan with the courgettes. Pour on the pesto, add the pine kernels and a little Parmesan cheese. Stir well to amalgamate everything, and serve in pre-heated bowls, with extra Parmesan for those who want it. Garnish each portion with a sprig of basil.

SERVES 2

# DOLCELATTE, LEEK AND LOVAGE SAUCE FOR PASTA

This sauce is rich and savoury, so is best served with plain cooked pasta, either fresh (page 70) or dried. It's also good on baked potatoes. All the dish needs by way of accompaniment is a crisp salad and a glass of cold dry white wine.

4 large leeks, cleaned, trimmed and sliced
15 g (½ oz) butter
170 ml (6 fl oz) dry white wine
salt
1 tablespoon finely-chopped fresh or frozen lovage leaves
90–110 g (3–4 oz) Dolcelatte cheese, cubed
60–90 g (2–3 oz) roasted pine kernels (see page 16 for roasting times)
grated fresh Parmesan cheese, to serve

In a wide, shallow pan, sweat the leeks for a few minutes in the melted butter. Add the wine and a little salt, cover the pan and simmer gently until the leeks are nearly cooked. Take off the lid, add the lovage leaves and allow the cooking liquid to reduce until it is syrupy and concentrated in flavour. Just before serving, stir in the cubed cheese and pine kernels.

Pour the sauce into drained hot pasta, stir and serve on warmed plates. Pass around the Parmesan for those who want it.

SERVES 2

# LEEKS AND FUSILLI WITH PESTO AND WHITE WINE

A fast, simple and delicious way of serving young leeks in their prime, this sauce, another of Andrew's recipes, is quite chunky and so is best served with pasta shapes such as *fusilli*, rather than spaghetti or noodles.

1 tablespoon of olive oil
15 g (½ oz) butter
1 onion, finely chopped
about 700g (1½ lb) leeks, sliced into 1 cm (½ inch) rounds
1 large clove of garlic, crushed
1 level teaspoon salt
1 generous glass (240 ml or 8 fl oz) of dry white wine
150 g (5 oz) dry, or 250 g (9 oz) of fresh pasta spirals or shells
about 60 g (2 oz) pesto, home-made (page 191) or bought
2 tablespoons full-fat Greek yogurt
freshly ground black pepper
fresh Parmesan cheese, grated

In a wide pan, heat the oil and butter, then fry the onion for a few minutes over a moderate heat. Add the leeks and garlic and fry for a few minutes longer. Add the salt, pour in the wine, turn up the heat and cook, shaking or stirring the pan until the wine has reduced by about half. Put on the lid, turn the heat down and stew the leeks until they are tender but not disintegrating. This will probably take around 20 minutes, but depends on the age and size of the leeks. When they are cooked, remove the lid and if the leeks seem watery just turn the heat up and allow the cooking liquid to reduce a little more.

Cook and drain your pasta according to the instructions on the packet, timing it to be ready at the same time as the leeks, or shortly afterwards.

When the leeks are cooked turn off the heat, stir in the pesto, yogurt, black pepper and cooked pasta. Serve in pre-warmed bowls and top with the Parmesan cheese. Garnish with a few fresh basil leaves if you have them.

SERVES 2

# PASTA WITH MUSHROOMS AND ROCKET

Thanks again to Andrew for this simple but delicious dish. He made it with wild rocket and very fresh Portabellini mushrooms, in well under half an hour. Proof, if any were needed, that you don't have to slave in the kitchen for hours to make something fabulous to eat (just get someone else to do it!).

1 tablespoon olive oil
150 g (5 oz) tiny button mushrooms, such as Portabellini, cleaned and left whole
70 g (2½ oz) rocket leaves, washed and dried
150 g (5 oz) dry or 250 g (9 oz) fresh pasta spirals
60 g (2 oz) pesto sauce, bought or home-made (page 191)
60 g (2 oz) fresh Parmesan cheese, grated
salt and freshly ground black pepper

Heat the oil and fry the mushrooms over a moderate heat for about 10 minutes, stirring or shaking the pan occasionally. Cut the rocket leaves into thirds, unless they are very tiny, in which case leave them whole.

Meanwhile cook the pasta in plenty of boiling salted water until *al dente*, then drain well.

Dilute the pesto sauce with 2–3 tablespoons of the pasta cooking water, until it is the consistency of double cream.

Now put the cooked pasta into the pan with the mushrooms, add the pesto, rocket and half the Parmesan cheese, and give it all a good stir. Add salt and pepper to taste, and serve immediately in warm bowls, with the rest of the Parmesan on top.

SERVES 2

# RED PEPPER AND ALMOND SAUCE FOR PASTA

This sauce is good with basic dry or fresh pasta, preferably one of the shapes such as spirals or shells. Due to its chunky texture it is less successful with noodles or spaghetti, as it is difficult to distribute evenly throughout the strands. It uses raw eggs, rather in the spirit of a Carbonara sauce, so be sure they are organic, free range and extremely fresh, and in the light of salmonella scares it probably should not be fed to the frail.

3 medium red peppers
2 onions, peeled and coarsely chopped
4 cloves of garlic, peeled and coarsely chopped
2 tablespoons olive oil
1 teaspoon balsamic vinegar
4 eggs
2 rounded tablespoons of finely chopped parsley
a little grated nutmeg
salt and freshly ground black pepper
310 g (11 oz) dry or 500 g (1 lb 2 oz) fresh pasta spirals
110 g (4 oz) blanched, roasted almonds (see page 16 for roasting times)
fresh Parmesan to serve – shavings or grated

Heat the oven to 220°C (425°F, gas 7) – adjust for fan ovens.

Wash, de-seed and dice the peppers into 2 cm (1 inch) squares. Coat the peppers, onion and garlic with the olive oil and balsamic vinegar, and place in a shallow baking dish in a single layer. Roast, uncovered, in the oven for 30–35 minutes until tender, turning them over about half way through the cooking time.

Meanwhile, beat the eggs in a bowl with the finely chopped parsley, a generous grating of nutmeg and some salt and pepper.

Cook the pasta in plenty of boiling salted water, timing it to be ready when the peppers finish roasting, drain well and return it to the pan in which it was cooked.

Stir the roasted vegetables and almonds into the drained, cooked pasta, then the eggs and a small handful of grated Parmesan. Serve in warm bowls and top each serving with extra Parmesan.

SERVES 4

# SAFFRON RAVIOLI FILLED WITH A PURÉE OF PETITS POIS

This is a delicate and sophisticated ravioli, with clean, bright flavours and lively colours. The pea purée is used both as the filling, and then thinned with cream and lemon juice to make a sauce for the ravioli. The pasta dough can be made in advance if necessary – it will keep in the fridge for a few days. Unless you make the filling very dry indeed, the ravioli is unlikely to keep successfully, as any moisture in the filling tends to seep into the pasta dough. It is better to fill the ravioli and cook it immediately.

Although the ravioli takes a while to fill, the purée is very easy and can even be made with frozen peas. This dish lends itself to production-line manufacture, so get some helpers, share out the wine left over from cooking, and make a social occasion of it.

PASTA
**Half quantity *Saffron pasta* (page 72)**

THE FILLING
**1 tablespoon olive oil**
**15 g (½ oz) butter**
**1 onion, finely chopped**
**450 g (1 lb) petits pois (prepared weight)**
**½ level teaspoon salt**
**240 ml (8 fl oz) dry white wine**
**grated rind of 1 washed lemon**
**freshly ground black pepper**

THE SAUCE
**surplus filling (about ⅓ of the total)**
**about 150 ml (5 fl oz) cream (single or double)**
**juice from about a quarter of lemon (to taste)**

TO SERVE
**a few roasted pine kernels to garnish (see page 16 for roasting times)**
**fresh Parmesan cheese, finely grated**

Make the saffron pasta as described on page 72, wrap in cling film or polythene and leave it to rest in the fridge.

THE FILLING

Heat the oil and butter together in a wide, shallow pan (a large frying pan is ideal) and sauté the onion gently for about 15 minutes, stirring, until softened and slightly browned. Turn up the heat, add the peas, salt and wine, stir in the grated lemon rind and cook with the pan uncovered for about 3 minutes, until the peas are tender, and the liquid considerably reduced.

Strain off the liquid into a jug and save it for later, place the peas and onions in a food processor or blender, add a few grinds of black pepper and whiz until smooth.

The purée should be quite stiff, and may need scraping down from the sides a couple of times. Leave it to cool while you roll out the pasta.

ASSEMBLY

Roll out the pasta quite thinly so that the finished ravioli won't be too heavy. Cut the pasta into 8–10 cm (3–4 inch) diameter circles using a sharp biscuit cutter. Don't be tempted to make the circles too small or they'll be difficult to fill. If you don't have a circular cutter, cut the pasta into squares using a ruler and a sharp knife. The trimmings can be re-kneaded and rolled as necessary, but may need spraying with a little water if they get too dry.

Fill the ravioli by putting a scant teaspoon of the pea purée in the centre of each circle. Don't overfill them or they may come apart during cooking. Moisten the edge of the pasta with your finger-tip dipped in cold water, fold in half, and seal firmly with your fingers, pressing out as much air as you can.

Lay the little half-moon parcels singly on a lightly-floured surface to dry, as you work. After a few minutes check to make sure the ravioli isn't sticking to the surface. If it is, turn it over. When all the ravioli is filled there should be about one third of the purée remaining.

THE SAUCE

Sieve the remaining pea purée into a clean saucepan, mix in the reserved cooking liquid and heat gently, stirring in some cream – enough to thin the purée to a pouring consistency. If you feel that too much cream would be needed (or you only have very thick cream), add a little hot water from the kettle. Stir in the lemon juice to taste – don't overdo it as the delicate pea flavour is easily swamped – and, finally, adjust the seasoning. Keep the sauce hot.

PUTTING IT ALL TOGETHER

Cook the ravioli in a large pan of boiling salted water for 3–4 minutes, until tender but still with some bite. Serve in warmed bowls, with a little of the hot sauce poured over. Garnish with a scattering of roasted pine kernels and pass round the freshly grated Parmesan cheese.

SERVES 3–4

# FRESH PARSLEY LASAGNE LAYERED WITH ROAST PUMPKIN AND CHARD

This is not a quick dish to make; however, virtually everything can be done well in advance, apart from the final baking. It makes an attractive autumn or winter dinner party dish, with its contrasting layers of green and orange. It is also comfort food *par excellence*.

ROASTED PUMPKIN SAUCE
about 2 kg (4 lb 5 oz) pumpkin (weighed before preparation)
a little olive oil
4 cloves of garlic, peeled
salt and freshly ground black pepper
up to 340 ml (12 fl oz) milk

CHARD SAUCE
1½ kg (3 lb) chard (weight includes stalks)
30 g (1 oz) butter
1 level teaspoon salt
2 level tablespoons plain flour
280 ml (10 fl oz) milk
juice of half a small lemon
200 g (7 oz) mature Cheddar cheese, grated

PARSLEY PASTA
1 recipe of herb pasta (page 71) made with fresh parsley
30 g (1 oz) pine kernels

Pre-heat the oven to 200°C (400°F, gas 6) – adjust for fan ovens

ROASTED PUMPKIN SAUCE

Halve the pumpkin using a sharp knife. Scrape out the seeds and fibre with a spoon and brush the cut surfaces and insides with a little olive oil. Place them cut sides down on an oiled baking tray. Put the whole, peeled garlic cloves under the pumpkins (in the cavity), and bake for about 30 minutes until tender.

Remove from the oven and leave until cool enough to handle, then scoop out the flesh, season with salt and pepper, and mash it with the garlic cloves.

The pumpkin mash needs to be wet enough to spread easily, so add milk during the mashing. The amount will depend on the type of pumpkin used, but may be anything up to 340 ml (12 fl oz).

CHARD SAUCE

Cut out and discard the thick ribs of the chard, but don't throw them away. You can use them in another recipe, or just steam them separately as a vegetable accompaniment for the lasagne.

Wash and coarsely chop the leaves. Wilt the leaves over a moderate heat in half the butter and add a level teaspoon of salt, then whiz them in the food processor.

In a large saucepan make a roux sauce using the remaining butter, the flour and milk. Follow the detailed instructions on page 184 if you need help with the method.

Cook the sauce for a few minutes, add the lemon juice, then season with salt and pepper. Remove it from the heat and stir in the grated cheese. When the cheese has melted, stir in the chard leaf purée.

PUTTING IT TOGETHER

Assemble the lasagne in a large rectangular dish. Roll out the pasta quite thinly, using a pasta machine, so the finished dish will not be too stodgy.

Spread a thin layer of chard sauce evenly over the bottom of the dish. Add a layer of pasta, making sure none of the sheets overlap, then a thin layer of pumpkin sauce, followed by another layer of pasta. Repeat the layers, until everything is used up, finishing with a layer of pumpkin sauce.

Ruffle the surface of the top pumpkin layer, using a fork.

Bake the lasagne for 20–25 minutes at 200°C (400°F, gas 6), until the top is nicely browned and the edges are bubbling.

About 10 minutes before the end of the cooking time, sprinkle the pine kernels over the top (don't do it any earlier or they'll burn).

SERVES 6–8

# SLOW-COOKED GREEK BEANS WITH TOMATOES, HERBS AND RED WINE

Saturated with intense flavour, these tender, plump beans are an example of peasant food *par excellence*. If you are lucky enough to find the huge, white 'giant beans' with which this dish is traditionally made, then snap them up and never mind the expense, but be sure to give them a long soak overnight. They need to absorb water and swell up before being cooked.

In Greece this dish is habitually baked all day long in the coolest part of a wood-fired oven – not very practical for most of us in the UK and elsewhere, but if you possess a slow-cooker (or an Aga), now is the time to use it. I cook the beans on top of the stove, but this requires a very solid pan, a low heat, and intermittent stirring to make sure they don't catch – no hassle, provided you're spending the day pottering around at home. The long, slow cooking is necessary for the full flavour of the dish to develop, and it's even better if you make it a day in advance.

The beans are traditionally served lukewarm, at which temperature their flavour is most intense.

250 g (9 oz) dried butter beans
2 tablespoons olive oil, plus extra for serving
4 medium onions, peeled and coarsely chopped
1 teaspoon dried mixed herbs or Greek oregano
3 large cloves of garlic, peeled and thinly sliced
450 g (1 lb) ripe tomatoes, peeled and chopped,
    or a 400 g (14 oz) tin of chopped tomatoes and juice
1 tablespoon sun-dried tomato paste
230 ml (8 fl oz) dry red wine
salt to taste

Soak the butter beans overnight in plenty of cold water. If you forget, pour boiling water on them, then leave to soak for at least 4 hours. *Should boil first!*

In a large, heavy pan or flame-proof casserole, warm the oil and sauté the onions and oregano for a few minutes. Add the garlic, tomatoes, tomato paste and wine.

Rinse the beans thoroughly in more cold water, then drain and add them to the pan. Stir well, and top up with a little water if necessary, so the beans are just submerged in liquid.

Bring it all to the boil, then turn the heat down until barely simmering, put a lid on the pan and cook as slowly as possible, stirring from time to time and adding extra boiling water if necessary, for between 6½ and 9 hours, until the beans are tender.

On a gas hob you may need a heat diffuser to get the temperature low enough.

Add salt only when the beans are tender, not before, as it would make them stay tough.

When the beans are cooked to your satisfaction, turn up the heat a little and cook uncovered for a while to reduce the sauce, but only if necessary.

Serve the beans lukewarm, with a little extra olive oil drizzled over them, accompanied by some good hot, crusty bread (or garlic bread), a crisp green side-salad and plenty of ice-cold retsina or rough red wine.

SERVES 3–4

# LENTILS COOKED IN RED WINE WITH MINT

This dish uses small green French Puy lentils, which are very tasty and less prone to disintegration than many other types. They have a lovely earthy quality, which is enlivened by the addition of mint and lemon late in the proceedings.

1 tablespoon olive oil
2 onions, coarsely chopped
1 red pepper, de-seeded and coarsely chopped
3 cloves of garlic, peeled and chopped
230 g (8 oz) Puy lentils, picked over and washed
230 ml (8 fl oz) of dry red wine
about 200 ml (7 fl oz) vegetable stock
½ a Habanero chilli, de-seeded and finely chopped
juice of half a lemon
1½ tablespoons shoyu, or other soy sauce
1 teaspoon balsamic vinegar
15 g (½ oz) fresh mint leaves, rolled up and cut into thin strips

In a large heavy pan, put the olive oil to warm over a medium heat. Sauté the onions, red pepper and garlic in the oil for about five minutes, stirring constantly. Throw in the washed and drained lentils, pour on the red wine and top up with the stock – just enough to cover the lentils. Put a lid on the pan and simmer gently for 25–35 minutes until the lentils are tender, stirring occasionally. If the pan seems to be drying out add a little boiling water or stock.

Put in the finely chopped chilli for the last 5 minutes of cooking time. With chillies, the 'heat' increases the longer you cook them. Since Habaneros are very fiery anyway, here they are given minimal cooking out of compassion for the diners. If you are using milder chillies you could put them in the pan at the beginning with the onions and red pepper.

Season the dish generously with the lemon juice, shoyu (or other soy sauce) and a splash of balsamic vinegar, and stir in the mint just before serving. Taste, and add extra salt if necessary.

Serve with mashed or baked potatoes, salad and a dollop of Greek yogurt or sour cream.

SERVES 3–4

# COUSCOUS WITH SAFFRON AND BUTTER BEANS

This is one of those slightly unusual recipes combining two different sorts of carbohydrate. It may seem a little strange, but for some reason it works very well – the beans and grain make perfect partners. The dish is warm, mild, soothing and savoury – good cold-weather food, and excellent teamed with something slightly astringent such as *Pink grapefruit and watercress salad* (page 53).

generous pinch of saffron threads
1 tablespoon olive oil
15 g (½ oz) butter (vegans substitute extra olive oil)
3 onions, peeled and coarsely chopped
3 cloves of garlic, peeled and chopped
250 g (9 oz) couscous
380 ml (13 fl oz) well-flavoured vegetable stock
400 g (14 oz) can of cooked butter beans, rinsed and drained
2 tablespoons finely chopped parsley or finely sliced chives

Put the saffron in a cup and pour on a couple of tablespoons of boiling water, then leave it to soak for at least 15 minutes. In a heavy saucepan, heat the oil and butter and fry the onions for about 10 minutes, stirring, over a moderate heat until they soften and start to go brown. Add the garlic, turn the heat down a little, and fry for a couple of minutes.

Add the couscous, stir thoroughly, then pour in the saffron liquid and vegetable stock. Cover the pan, and simmer without stirring on the lowest possible heat for 10 minutes, until all the stock is absorbed. If any liquid remains simply leave the pan on a very low heat for a few minutes longer.

Using a fork, gently fluff up the couscous and stir in the rinsed and drained butter beans and the chopped parsley or chives. Heat gently for a couple of minutes, until the butter beans are heated through, then taste, add salt and pepper if necessary, and serve.

SERVES 3

VARIATION
This dish is also nice made with chick peas instead of butter beans.

# SWEET-POTATO PIE WITH PUY LENTILS IN A WINE SAUCE

This is a sort of slightly posh, vegetarian version of Shepherd's Pie. The sweet potatoes could be replaced with ordinary potatoes if you wanted to remain truer to the spirit of the original.

With its combination of western and eastern ingredients the recipe is, I suppose, an example of the much-hyped 'fusion' cooking – something vegetarians have been quietly getting on with for decades.

15 g (½ oz) dried ceps or other dried mushrooms
110 g (4 oz) Puy lentils
700 g (1½ lb) sweet potatoes
salt and freshly ground black pepper
110 g (4 oz) mature Cheddar cheese, grated (omit for vegans)
2 medium red onions, peeled and chopped
3–4 stalks celery, sliced
1 cm (½ inch) cube fresh ginger, peeled and chopped
1 large or 2 small sweet red peppers, de-seeded
   and cut into 2 cm (1 inch) squares
1 tablespoon olive oil
1 fresh red chilli, chopped (more if you like)
2 cloves garlic, peeled and chopped
230 ml (8 fl oz) dry red wine
about 280 ml (10 fl oz) vegetable stock
2 rounded teaspoons sun-dried tomato paste
1 tablespoon chopped fresh lovage leaves
   (use celery leaves if you can't get lovage)
30 g (1 oz) fresh bread-crumbs

Oven temperature: 200°C (400°F, gas 6) – adjust for fan ovens

Rinse the dried mushrooms in cold water, then soak in a little boiling water for 15–25 minutes. Wash, pick over and drain the lentils.

Peel and cook the sweet potatoes in boiling salted water until tender – about 15–20 minutes, depending on their size.

Drain, add salt and pepper, and mash them, adding all but 2 tablespoons of the grated cheese. Use a potato masher or a fork, but don't put them in the food processor as it will spoil the texture.

In a large, heavy, lidded frying pan sauté the onions, celery, ginger and red pepper in the olive oil for a few minutes.

Add the lentils, chilli and garlic to the pan, stir, and pour in the dried mushrooms with their soaking water. Add the red wine and enough stock just to cover the lentils. Bring it all to the boil, turn the heat down, cover and simmer for 20–35 minutes until the lentils are tender.

If much liquid remains, remove the lid, turn the heat up and allow the liquid to reduce for a few minutes – the lentils should be in a little sauce, not a swamp.

Stir in the sun-dried tomato paste and lovage leaves, taste, and adjust the seasoning if necessary. Tip the contents of the pan into an oven-proof baking or gratin dish.

Spread the mashed sweet potato and cheese mixture on the top. Mix the reserved cheese with the bread crumbs and sprinkle on top of the sweet potatoes.

Note: to jazz this dish up a bit for vegans, add some chopped walnuts to the bread crumb topping.

If you want to prepare the dish in advance you can, at this point, cool, cover and refrigerate (or even freeze) it before the final baking, but don't (as I once did) put a ceramic or Pyrex dish straight from a cold fridge into a hot oven – it may shatter.

Bake for 20–30 minutes in the pre-heated oven until nicely browned on top.

SERVES 4

# TERRINE OF CASHEWS, ALMONDS AND APPLES

Although the idea of a nut loaf seems rather old-fashioned these days, it's useful to have a good one in the repertoire, if only to fill that turkey-shaped hole in the menu at Christmas or Thanksgiving! This one is lighter than most and looks very festive, flecked with jewel-like redcurrants and with an apple ring in the centre of each slice.

You get the apple ring effect by burying a 'pipe-line' of cored, filled apples, end to end in the middle of the loaf. The number of apples needed depends on their size and on the length of your terrine. It's essential to use *small* or trimmed-down apples and a deep but narrow terrine, otherwise there won't be enough nut mixture to bury the apples properly and you'll end up with something that looks like the Loch Ness monster! For the same reason, don't leave out any of the ingredients (such as the redcurrants).

Serve the terrine with all your favourite roast dinner trimmings, such as *Red onion and redcurrant relish* (page 194) and *Onion sauce with Marsala* (page 186).

1 large onion, peeled and finely chopped
4 stalks celery, finely chopped
2 cm (1 inch) cube fresh ginger, peeled and thinly sliced
1 tablespoon butter
1 teaspoon olive oil
3 cloves of garlic, peeled and finely chopped
½ a fresh Habanero chilli, or equivalent
230 ml (8 fl oz) dry white wine
1 level teaspoon salt
freshly ground black pepper
200 g (7 oz) blanched almonds, roasted (see page 16 for roasting times)
140 g (5 oz) unsalted cashew pieces, roasted
1 slice of white bread, made into crumbs
3 tablespoons parsley, finely chopped
110 g (4 oz) redcurrants, fresh or frozen
2 eggs, lightly beaten
3 or 4 small apples, preferably Cox's Orange Pippins, Egremont Russets,
   or other characterful dessert apples

Oven temperature: 190°C (375°F, gas 5) – adjust for fan ovens

In a large, heavy frying pan sauté the onions, celery and ginger in the butter and olive oil over a moderate heat for 10–15 minutes – add the garlic for the last minute or so.

Add the fresh chilli and the wine, bring to the boil, then turn down the heat and simmer uncovered for 10–15 minutes, until the wine is reduced by about two thirds, then take the pan off the heat. Add the salt and some freshly ground black pepper, and leave on one side to cool slightly.

Whiz all the roasted almonds and about half the cashews in a food processor, until they are coarsely ground. Leave a little texture, but no big chunks. Some of the cashew pieces are left whole for textural contrast.

When the frying pan has cooled down, add all the nuts and the bread-crumbs to the vegetable and wine mixture. Stir in the parsley, redcurrants and beaten eggs. Taste, and adjust the seasoning if necessary. If the mixture seems unmanageably stiff, thin it with a little milk or cream.

Butter the sides and line the base of a deep, narrow 1lb loaf tin or terrine, using non-stick baking parchment.

Pre-heat the oven if you haven't already done so.

Peel and core the apples and cut a slice off both top and bottom to give flat surfaces. Carefully trim the outsides of each apple parallel to the core hole so as to end up with sections of apple 'pipe' about 5 cm (2 inches) in diameter.

Chop the apple trimmings finely and add them to the nut mixture. Fill the apple core cavities with some of the nut mixture, pressing it down gently.

Now spread a 2 cm (1 inch) layer of nut mixture in the loaf tin and lay your apple pipe-line in a row end to end on top of it, with the core-holes aligned and running lengthwise through the centre of the loaf. Bed the apples down a little into the nut mixture to anchor them firmly. Pack the remaining filling around and over the apples, firming it into place with your fingers. Level the top with a knife and cover it loosely with a piece of buttered aluminium foil.

Bake in the pre-heated oven for 45 minutes, then remove the foil and bake for 15 minutes more, or until firm.

Remove the terrine from the oven and leave it to cool in the tin for a few minutes, then loosen around the sides with a knife. Turn out the terrine by inverting a large plate over the top of the tin, holding the tin and plate together and turning everything upside down. Peel off the lining paper carefully. Slice and serve hot or lukewarm.

SERVES 8

# REFRITOS

Although not desperately authentic, my re-fried beans have some good Mexican flavours. Strictly speaking they are re-baked rather than re-fried, since I heat them through in the oven to minimize the use of fat. The beans can be used as a filling for tortillas, burritos, etc., as part of a Mexican meal, which might also include *Fresh tomato and pepper salsa* (page 28), *Guacamole* (page 54), and a bowl of sour cream.

2 × 400g (14 oz) cans of pre-cooked pinto beans in brine or water,
   or 250 g (9 oz) dried pinto beans
3 tablespoons olive oil
250 g (9 oz) red onions, peeled and chopped
3 cloves garlic, peeled and crushed
1 Habanero chilli, or 2 of a less fierce type, de-seeded and finely chopped
1 level teaspoon salt
2 large ripe tomatoes, diced
squeeze of fresh lemon juice
generous handful of fresh coriander leaves, washed and coarsely chopped

If you are using dried beans soak them in water, overnight preferably, but if you forget, then pour boiling water on them and leave for at least 1 hour, so they can absorb some water and soften slightly before cooking. The next day, drain and rinse the beans, then cook them in fresh, un-salted water. Fast-boil for 10 minutes, then turn the heat down and simmer for 40 minutes or more, until they are tender. The exact time will depend on the age and condition of the beans, so keep testing. They need to be quite soft.

Drain the beans, return them to the pan and mash with a potato masher, pestle or fork. Don't worry if there are a few lumps. If using canned beans, drain and rinse them, then mash as for dried.

While the beans are cooking heat the oil in a small saucepan. Fry the onion over a moderate heat, stirring occasionally, for 15–20 minutes. Add the garlic, chilli and salt and cook for a couple of minutes more. Stir in the tomatoes and remove the pan from the heat immediately – the tomatoes should not be cooked.

Stir the vegetables and lemon juice into the mashed beans, mixing well, then stir in the chopped coriander. Taste, and add extra salt if necessary.

To re-heat, place the beans in an oven-proof dish, cover tightly in foil and heat through in the oven. Garnish with thick wedges of lime, chilli rings and an extra scattering of coriander leaves before serving.

SERVES 4–6

# RISOTTO

Risotto is one of my ultimate comfort foods, creamy, fragrant and inviting. The single most important factor in making a decent risotto is the rice. It is impossible to make the dish correctly without proper Italian risotto rice of some sort - the two most commonly available are *arborio* and *carnaroli*. They have the capacity to stand up to much stirring and absorb liquid without disintegrating. Risotto is best made in a wide, shallow pan with a heavy base.

The basic cooking method is quite straightforward, and once grasped is easily varied. Usually but not always (see the note below about fragile ingredients) the vegetables chosen for flavouring are first sautéed in a mixture of butter and olive oil, then the rice is added and sautéed with them. At this point wine is often added. It's not absolutely essential, but is a great asset. The rice is cooked and stirred for a while, until much of the wine has evaporated leaving behind just concentrated flavour.

Vegetable stock is kept simmering in a pan on the back of the stove and added to the rice about a ladleful at a time, as the risotto continues to cook over a medium heat. The rice is stirred frequently to prevent sticking, especially towards the end of the cooking time, and as the liquid is absorbed and the pan dries out, more stock is added as necessary until cooking is complete. The idea is to have nearly all the liquid absorbed by the time the rice is done. When cooked, the dish should be creamy and the rice soft but still with a little bite in the centre of each grain. This takes about 20 minutes from the time liquid is first added.

The dish is finished usually by the addition of fresh herbs, often a little extra butter or cream and, more often than not, freshly grated Parmesan cheese.

### FRAGILE INGREDIENTS

If you are using a delicate vegetable, such as asparagus, that may not stand up well to prolonged cooking and stirring, cook it separately and combine it with the rice just before serving. This has the added advantage of allowing precise timing of both vegetable and rice, and if you cook the vegetable first, its cooking water can be used in the risotto stock. When using this method I invariably add onion and garlic to the basic risotto, to ensure the rice absorbs some flavour during cooking.

### VEGETABLE STOCK – HOME-MADE VERSUS INSTANT

I have already dwelt on this quandary in the introduction so I won't go over the same ground too much. The quality of the stock has a big impact on the final flavour of most risottos, so for a special risotto you may prefer to use home-made stock. The stock flavouring can then be tailored to the recipe for which it is intended. A good general recipe is given on page 208. Some of the better supermarkets sell fresh vegetable stock, at a price. For everyday risottos I use my favourite instant stock powder – Marigold Swiss Vegetable Bouillon.

## VEGETABLE STOCK – A SNEAKY SHORTCUT

Rather than having a separate pan of stock simmering on the stove, I usually put as much stock powder as I think I will need straight into the risotto pan at the point where stock would first be added to the rice, then add boiling water from the electric kettle as necessary. Bear in mind that since much of the water will evaporate during cooking the stock flavour will intensify, so err on the side of caution initially, especially if using a concentrate.

# LEEK AND MUSHROOM RISOTTO

This is an uncomplicated and savoury risotto, using ingredients readily available almost anywhere.

10 g (¼ oz) dried mushrooms, preferably ceps
15 g (½ oz) butter
1 tablespoon olive oil
1 onion, peeled and chopped
250 g (9 oz) leeks (prepared weight), cut into 5 mm (¼ inch) slices
200 g (7 oz) mushrooms, cleaned and cut into chunks
    unless very tiny, in which case leave them whole
3 cloves of garlic, peeled and finely chopped
110 g (4 oz) arborio or other risotto rice
170 ml (6 fl oz) dry white wine
about 300 ml (10 fl oz) vegetable stock
fresh Parmesan cheese, grated

If you are unfamiliar with the risotto-making technique, some detailed instructions are given on page 93.

Put the dried mushrooms to soak in a bowl with just enough boiling water to cover them. Leave at least 20 minutes (45 would be better), then strain the liquid into a jug by pouring it through a very fine sieve or paper coffee filter. Rinse the drained mushrooms under running water to remove any debris, then chop them finely.

Put the butter and olive oil into a large, heavy pan, and sauté the chopped onion over a moderate heat, stirring. After a couple of minutes add the leeks and fresh mushrooms. After a few minutes more add the chopped dried mushrooms, the garlic and the rice. Give it a stir, then pour in the wine and allow it to bubble and reduce a bit.

Pour in the reserved mushroom soaking water and top up with enough simmering vegetable stock to just cover the rice. Simmer, stirring when necessary, and keep adding a little extra simmering stock if the rice seems to be sticking. The rice takes about 20 minutes to cook, by which time you should aim to have nearly all the liquid absorbed. Taste, and season if necessary. Stir a handful of grated Parmesan cheese into the risotto before serving and pass round extra Parmesan at the table.

SERVES 2

# MUSHROOM RISOTTO WITH MARSALA

I'm lucky in having a local supplier of unusual organically-grown mushrooms, so often make this risotto with a mixture of very fresh shiitake and pink oyster mushrooms, with consistently good results. When I've had to substitute non-organic equivalents from the supermarket the flavour was definitely inferior. Whether it's the organic factor, the freshness factor or a combination of the two I don't know. Whatever, use a selection of the very best mushrooms you can find.

The recipe uses two very different wines in different stages of the cooking, a sweet Marsala and a dry white table wine, and the contrast when the two elements of the dish are eventually brought together is a happy one. If you can find really good mushrooms the alcoholic extravagance is well justified.

10 g (¼ oz) dried mushrooms, preferably ceps or shiitake
450 g (1 lb) mixed fresh mushrooms – 2 or 3 different sorts
30 g (1 oz) butter
2 tablespoons olive oil
1 onion, chopped
1 large clove of garlic, finely chopped
110 g (4 oz) risotto rice
170 ml (6 fl oz) of dry white wine
about 300 ml (10 fl oz) vegetable stock, not too strongly-flavoured
juice of half a lemon
salt and freshly ground black pepper
170 ml (6 fl oz) sweet Marsala
2 heaped tablespoons chopped chives
2 or 3 tablespoons fresh cream (optional)
fresh grated Parmesan cheese to serve

Put the dried mushrooms to soak in a bowl with just enough boiling water to cover them. Leave at least 20 minutes (45 would be better), then strain through a very fine sieve or coffee filter, saving the liquid. Rinse the drained mushrooms under running water to remove any grit, then chop them finely.

Clean and cut up the fresh mushrooms, into reasonably large pieces. If using fresh shiitake mushrooms, you may want to discard the stalks, which can be rather tough (alternatively, just chop them very finely).

Put half the butter and olive oil into a large pan, and sauté the chopped onion over a moderate heat. After a few minutes add the chopped dried mushrooms, the garlic and the rice. Give it a stir, then pour in the white wine and allow it to bubble and reduce a bit.

Pour in the reserved mushroom soaking water and top up with enough vegetable stock to just cover the rice. Simmer, stirring when necessary, and keep adding a little extra simmering stock if the rice seems to be sticking. The rice takes about 20 minutes to cook, by the end of which time you should aim to have nearly all the liquid absorbed. Taste, and season if necessary.

Meanwhile put the rest of the butter and olive oil in a separate large frying pan and sauté the fresh mushrooms briskly. When they sizzle and start to brown, pour in the lemon juice. Keep the heat quite brisk throughout. Add a little salt and, as the lemon juice evaporates, add the Marsala in stages. Don't add it all at once, or the mushrooms will go soggy.

The idea is basically to fry the mushrooms, keeping everything quite dry, but with the addition of some well-flavoured liquid from time to time, to stop the mushrooms from sticking and add a bit of oomph. If you want to make double quantity, fry the mushrooms in batches to stop them going soggy.

They should be browned and cooked in about 15 minutes, and be ready at the same time as the rice. The relatively high cooking temperature drives off much of the water, and concentrates the flavours.

When both mushrooms and rice are cooked, you have two options. If omitting the cream, stir the chopped chives directly into the rice. Pile the rice on warmed plates and top with the fried mushrooms. If using the cream, stir the chives into it and pour a little over each portion of rice, before topping with the mushrooms. Either way, pass round the Parmesan cheese.

SERVES 2

# PUMPKIN RISOTTO WITH SAFFRON

This warming dish of fragrant, saffron-infused rice, studded with sweet orange chunks of pumpkin, is a delight to the senses. The texture is creamy and soothing; the colour like a burst of sunshine on the plate – just the thing for a dismal autumn or winter day.

Saffron, the dried stamens of the saffron crocus, is the world's costliest spice, but a little goes a long way, and it adds immeasurably to the quality of this, and any other dish in which it plays a part. There is no adequate substitute. If you're going to the expense, buy it whole rather than powdered. After opening, store it in an airtight container in the fridge.

This dish can be made with any orange-fleshed winter pumpkin or squash. Given the choice I make it with butternut squash, which has a good flavour, comes in a manageable size, and is easy to peel.

a generous pinch of saffron strands
700 g (1 lb 9 oz) prepared pumpkin (buy about a third extra to allow for wastage)
30 g (1 oz) butter
1 tablespoon olive oil
1 medium onion, finely chopped
170 g (6 oz) risotto rice
360 ml (12 fl oz) dry white wine
about 600 ml (21 fl oz) vegetable stock, not too strongly flavoured
2 heaped tablespoons finely chopped parsley
grated fresh Parmesan cheese to serve
salt and freshly ground black pepper
2 or 3 tablespoons of cream or crème fraîche (optional)
a few toasted pumpkin seeds for garnishing (optional)

Put the saffron threads to soak in about 2 tablespoons of boiling water for at least 10 minutes.

Prepare the pumpkin or squash by first cutting it in half lengthwise (it helps if your knife is large and very sharp, since stored pumpkins can have very tough skin). As a last resort if you really can't get the knife in, drop the pumpkin on a hard floor from about shoulder height.

Scoop out the seeds and fibres with a spoon, and discard them. Now place the pumpkin halves cut-side down and cut into slices 1 cm (½ inch) wide. Put each slice flat (cut side) on the chopping board and slice off the skin with a few swift downward strokes of the knife.

Cut the pumpkin flesh into approximately 1 cm (½ inch) dice. Don't make them too much bigger than this, as they need to be cooked through in the same time as it takes for the rice to get tender.

Heat the butter and olive oil together in a large shallow pan; when the butter is foaming throw in the pumpkin. Shake the pan from time to time, to prevent sticking. The heat should be quite high, as the aim is to brown the pumpkin slightly before the main part of the cooking takes place. This should only take 2–3 minutes. The butter will caramelise slightly, which adds to the flavour.

Turn the pieces over gently, and when they are slightly coloured, reduce the heat a little and add the onions. After a few minutes more, add the rice, followed by the wine. Allow it to bubble and reduce for a few minutes. Add the saffron and its soaking liquid.

Begin adding simmering vegetable stock and continue cooking the risotto as described on page 93, until the rice is tender and virtually all the liquid is absorbed – about 20 minutes from the time the liquid is first added.

Just before serving, stir in the chopped parsley and a handful of grated Parmesan cheese. Add plenty of black pepper, taste and add extra salt if necessary – if the vegetable stock was salty you may not need any. Top each portion with a dollop of cream or crème fraîche. Garnish with a few toasted pumpkin seeds if you have any, and serve with extra Parmesan.

SERVES 3–4

# QUINOA WITH BRAISED MEDITERRANEAN VEGETABLES, HERBS AND GOAT'S CHEESE

Quinoa makes an interesting accompaniment, delicate but savoury, to what is essentially a variation on ratatouille – a dish of slow-cooked summer vegetables. The braised vegetables take considerably longer to cook than the quinoa, so get them well underway first. Serve the two dishes side by side. They taste good individually, as well as in combination.

### THE BRAISED VEGETABLES

2 medium onions
1 large or 2 small red peppers
1 medium sized aubergine
2 tablespoons olive oil
chopped leaves from 2 sprigs fresh rosemary
½ tablespoon fresh lemon thyme leaves
1 clove of garlic, peeled and thinly sliced
salt
3 heaped teaspoons of sun-dried tomato paste
12 Kalamata olives, stones removed
6 generous tablespoons of creamy goat's cheese

### THE QUINOA

2 medium onions, peeled and chopped
1 tablespoon olive oil
15 g (½ oz) butter
170 g (6 oz) quinoa
1 clove of garlic, peeled and chopped
120 ml (4 fl oz) vegetable stock
2 tablespoons finely chopped parsley

### THE BRAISED VEGETABLES

To cook the vegetables you will need a large, heavy frying pan with a well-fitting lid.

Cut the onions into long narrow strips, the pepper into 2 cm (1 inch) squares and the aubergine first lengthwise into quarters and then into hefty chunks.

Warm the olive oil over a moderate heat in the frying pan. Add the prepared vegetables, rosemary and lemon thyme. Swirl them around and sauté for a few minutes before adding the garlic and about 1 teaspoon of salt.

The vegetables will probably stick slightly, so add a splash or two of boiling water from the kettle. Cover the pan, turn the heat down and simmer for about 35 minutes until the vegetables are quite tender, stirring occasionally and adding a little hot water from time to time, if anything seems to be sticking or drying out too much.

Meanwhile, put the sun-dried tomato paste in a cup and dilute with a small amount of hot water, until it is the consistency of double cream. While the vegetables are cooking, get the quinoa underway.

## THE QUINOA

Fry the onion in the olive oil and butter over a moderate heat for about 15 minutes, stirring occasionally, until it is golden brown. Meanwhile, put the quinoa in a fine sieve and rinse thoroughly in cold water to remove any bitterness.

Add the garlic to the onions and fry for a couple of minutes. Add the quinoa to the pan, stir well, and pour in the vegetable stock. You may need to add salt at this stage, depending on how salty your stock is.

Bring the quinoa to the boil, then turn the heat down to the lowest setting. Cover the pan and simmer for 15 minutes, stirring occasionally. Remove the lid and, if there is any liquid remaining, just leave the pan on the heat uncovered for a few minutes to allow it to evaporate.

Fluff up the grains with a fork and stir in the chopped parsley before serving.

## FINISHING THE BRAISED VEGETABLES

Take the lid off the frying pan, add the tomato paste and the olives and stir (carefully, to prevent total vegetable disintegration). If the vegetables seem at all watery, leave the pan on a moderate heat with the lid off for a few minutes to allow some steam to escape.

Finally, dot generous dollops of creamy goat's cheese over the vegetables, turn off the heat and put the lid back on the pan for a few minutes to melt the cheese.

SERVES 2–3

# RISOTTO OF LEEKS, PETITS POIS AND PINE KERNELS

Here is another risotto made from quite basic ingredients, which shouldn't be too hard to find. I generally use frozen peas in this recipe, which makes it very quick.

1 tablespoon olive oil
15 g (½ oz) butter
4–6 leeks, trimmed, cleaned and sliced
110 g (4 oz) Arborio or other risotto rice
2 tablespoons chopped lovage (or parsley)
170 ml (6 fl oz) dry white wine
about 300 ml (10 fl oz) vegetable stock
200 g (7 oz) petits pois, fresh or frozen (weight after shelling)
60 g (2 oz) roasted pine kernels (see page 16 for roasting times)
fresh grated Parmesan cheese to serve

Warm the oil and butter in a large, heavy pan. Sauté the leeks for a few minutes until they begin to soften. Add the rice and swirl it about so it's well coated in the oil and butter mixture. Throw in the chopped lovage, followed by the wine, and let it bubble and reduce slightly.

Begin adding the stock and continue cooking as described on page 93, for about 15 minutes.

Add the petits pois, bring the risotto back to the boil and cook for a further 5 minutes, until the rice is tender and the liquid absorbed.

Stir in the roasted pine kernels at the very last minute before serving, to retain their crispness. Pass the fresh Parmesan around separately.

SERVES 2

# HERB COUSCOUS

This fragrant, herby couscous makes a good accompaniment to a dish of roast or sautéed vegetables. As herbs vary in intensity of flavour, so, accordingly, do the amounts given in the suggestions below.

1 large onion, peeled and chopped
1 tablespoon olive oil
15 g (½ oz) butter (vegans substitute olive oil)
2 cloves of garlic, crushed
250 g (9 oz) couscous
380 ml (13 fl oz) well-flavoured vegetable stock
salt and freshly ground black pepper
1 or 2 tablespoons of chopped fresh herbs – see below for suggestions

You need a pan with a well-fitting lid for this recipe.

Sauté the onions in the olive oil and butter over a medium heat until they are softened and slightly browned. Add the garlic just for the last couple of minutes of the onion cooking time, to avoid burning it, then stir in the couscous.

Pour in the boiling vegetable stock and stir gently with a fork, to break up the lumps of couscous, then cover the pan with a lid, turn the heat down as low as it will go, and cook very, very gently for about 15 minutes. If the base of your pan is rather thin, or your heat at all fierce, use a heat diffuser, or the couscous will catch.

Taste for seasoning and add salt if necessary, then gently fork in the chopped herbs, breaking up any lumps in the couscous as you do so.

SERVES 3, GENEROUSLY

HERB VARIATIONS

- 2 tablespoons of chopped basil, if serving with a dish containing tomatoes.
- 2 tablespoons of lemon thyme, if serving with *Roasted Mediterranean Vegetables* (page 113).
- 1 tablespoon of chopped lovage, to accompany a celery or celeriac dish.
- 1 tablespoon of finely-chopped rosemary, to serve with *Red onions with Seville orange and Marsala* (page 137).
- 2 tablespoons of parsley, chives or Welsh onion greens to go with almost any dish that doesn't have a more obvious herb partner.

# TARRAGON COUSCOUS WITH ROASTED PUMPKIN

A variation on the preceding recipe, this is a nice dish of simple, clean flavours for springtime or early summer, when the new tarragon has emerged in the garden and there are still some good pumpkins and winter squashes available from storage. I often make it with butternut squash, as they are easy to obtain, tasty and a manageable size, but any well-flavoured pumpkin or winter squash will do.

Although I usually serve the dish with Parmesan cheese, this (and the small quantity of butter used in the cooking) can be omitted to make the dish completely vegan, in which case add a scattering of roasted pine kernels to garnish.

If you're not sure how to deal with a whole pumpkin, an easy method is given in the recipe for *Pumpkin risotto with saffron* on page 98.

about 700 g (1½ lb) of pumpkin (see note above),
   peeled and cut into 2 cm (1 inch) chunks
2 tablespoons olive oil
salt and freshly ground black pepper
1 onion, peeled and chopped
15 g (½ oz) butter (vegans substitute olive oil)
1 clove of garlic, crushed
250 g (9 oz) couscous
380 ml (13 fl oz) vegetable stock
a pinch of saffron threads, softened in 2 tablespoons of boiling water
1 tablespoon of chopped fresh French tarragon
to serve: freshly-grated Parmesan cheese (vegans omit)
   or a few roasted pine kernels, but not both

Pre-heat the oven to 240°C (460°F, gas 9) – adjust for fan ovens.

Toss the pumpkin chunks in 1 tablespoon of the olive oil and a little salt. Place them in a baking tray in a single layer, uncovered, and roast in the hot oven. Stir once, half way through the cooking time (about 20 minutes in total, although the exact time depends on the type of pumpkin used). The pumpkin chunks should be tender but not disintegrating.

Meanwhile, sauté the onions in the remaining olive oil and butter over a medium heat until they are softened and slightly browned. Add the garlic (just for the last couple of minutes of the onion cooking time to avoid burning it), then stir in the couscous. Add the vegetable stock and stir gently with a fork to break up the lumps of couscous, then cover the pan with a lid, turn the heat down as low as it will go, and cook very gently for about 15 minutes, stirring occasionally with a fork. About half way through the 15 minutes fork in the saffron and its liquid.

Taste for seasoning and add salt if necessary, then just before serving, stir in the chopped tarragon. Serve with the roasted pumpkin on the side, and pass around freshly grated Parmesan cheese for those who want it.

SERVES 3

# BAKED SPICED POLENTA WITH A FRESH TOMATO SAUCE

Polenta as it is commonly prepared can be a trifle bland or, at any rate, overly reliant on large amounts of butter and cheese for flavouring. In an attempt to jolly it up without bringing on a heart attack I added fresh Habanero chilli and lemon juice, as well as rather more modest quantities of butter and cheese than is often recommended.

230 g (8 oz) polenta
1 level teaspoon salt
270 ml (9 fl oz) cold water
500 ml (18 fl oz) hot water
1 fresh red chilli, finely chopped
30 g (1 oz) butter
110 g (4 oz) fresh grated Parmesan cheese
freshly ground black pepper
juice of half a lemon
double quantity of *Summer tomato sauce with basil and cream* (page 193).

Oven temperature: 220°C (425°F, gas 7) – adjust for fan ovens

Using a fork mix the polenta and salt with the cold water in a jug. In a large pan, bring the measured volume of hot water to a rolling boil. Stir the polenta sludge into the boiling water using a long-handled wooden spoon. It will soon thicken quite dramatically and start to plop like molten lava, so stand back. Reduce the heat and simmer for 15 minutes, stirring occasionally.

Add the chopped chilli and cook for another 5 minutes, then take the pan off the heat and stir in the butter, Parmesan and lemon juice. Taste, and add more lemon juice, salt and pepper, if necessary.

Spread the polenta into an oiled dish (something about the size and shape of a small loaf tin is about right). If you don't have the right sort of container just tip it onto a sheet of silicon paper, oil your hands and use them to shape it roughly into a brick. Leave the polenta to cool for at least 1 hour, after which it will be set solid and sliceable.

Pre-heat the oven now if you haven't already done so.

Turn the polenta onto a chopping board and cut into 5 mm (¼ inch) slices with a very sharp knife. If it sticks or crumbles try oiling the knife blade, and/or chilling the polenta for a while. The slices may be cut into squares, triangles or any other shape you fancy. Spread them out in a single layer on oiled baking trays or shallow dishes and bake for about 10–12 minutes until brown and crispy. They may run slightly, but it doesn't really matter.

Serve hot with the hot, creamy sauce.

SERVES 3–4

# BAKED POLENTA LAYERED WITH THREE SAUCES

Three sauces make this sound like rather an epic, but this dish is not as hard to make as it sounds, since the sauces are individually quite simple and can be prepared in advance. It makes a nice autumn dinner party dish, substantial and impressive, and needs only a crisp salad and some good bread by way of accompaniment.

### THE POLENTA

230 g (8 oz) polenta
½ level teaspoon of salt
770 ml (27 fl oz) water
juice of half a lemon
90 g (3 oz) fresh Parmesan cheese,
    finely grated

### ROASTED ONION SAUCE

450 g (1 lb) red onions
450 g (1 lb) ordinary onions
450 g (1 lb) shallots
12 cloves of garlic
leaves from
    3 branches of fresh rosemary
    or 12 branches of lemon thyme,
    washed and chopped
salt and freshly ground black pepper
2 tablespoons olive oil
230 ml (8 fl oz) dry white wine

### TOMATO SAUCE

about 1 kg (2 lb) fresh tomatoes,
    peeled and chopped
1 tablespoon olive oil
1 level teaspoon salt
3 cloves of garlic, peeled and chopped
12–15 fresh basil leaves

### CHEESE SAUCE

15 g (½ oz) butter
1 level tablespoon flour
150 ml (5 fl oz) milk
170 g (6 oz) strong Cheddar cheese
    or 90 g (3 oz) fresh Parmesan, grated
squeeze of fresh lemon juice
¼ teaspoon of Dijon mustard
salt and freshly ground black pepper

### CRISP TOPPING

60 g (2 oz) grated Cheddar cheese
1 slice-worth of fresh bread crumbs

Oven temperature: 200°C (400°F, gas 6) – adjust for fan ovens

### THE POLENTA

Mix the polenta and salt with 230 ml (8 fl oz) of the water, and boil the rest of the water in a large pan. Stir the polenta sludge into the boiling water. For safety's sake use a long-handled wooden spoon, as when the mixture thickens it plops and spits. Turn the heat down and simmer, stirring occasionally, until cooked – the time will vary according to the type of polenta you are using, so follow any timing instructions on the packet. While it is still hot stir in the lemon juice and Parmesan cheese.

Tip the mixture into an oiled rectangular dish or mould, or shape it into a brick, and leave aside to cool. When you've made the sauces and are ready to assemble the dish, turn it onto a chopping board and slice as thinly as possible with a very sharp, oiled knife. You will probably need to clean the blade between slices.

Pre-heat the oven if you haven't already done so.

## ROASTED ONION SAUCE

Peel the onions (both kinds), shallots and garlic cloves. You can speed up the peeling process by blanching them in boiling water for a minute or two, to loosen the skins. Quarter the onions (unless they're huge in which case cut them into eighths), halve the shallots and leave the garlic whole. Put them all in a roasting tin with the herbs, season with salt and pepper, and coat everything in the olive oil, turning it all over with your fingers to ensure an even coating. Add the wine, then bake, covered for about 30 minutes, then uncovered for another 10 (40 minutes in total).

## TOMATO SAUCE

Make a fast-cooked tomato sauce by frying the peeled, chopped tomatoes in the olive oil in a large frying pan. Add the salt and garlic during the cooking and use a brisk heat. The idea is to cook off quite a lot of the liquid fairly rapidly, to concentrate the tomato flavour. When the sauce looks quite well-reduced take it off the heat and stir in the chopped basil.

## CHEESE SAUCE

In a small saucepan, make a roux sauce using the butter, flour and milk. Follow the detailed instructions on page 184 if you need help with the method. Simmer the sauce (continuing to stir) for a few minutes to cook the flour. Take the pan off the heat and stir in the cheese, lemon juice and mustard, then season to taste with salt and pepper.

## PUTTING IT ALL TOGETHER

Reduce the oven temperature to 180°C (350°F, gas 4) – adjust for fan ovens.

Layer the polenta slices, tomato sauce and onion sauce in your lasagne dish: polenta, tomato, polenta, onion, polenta, tomato, etc., starting and ending with polenta.

Spread the cheese sauce over the final layer of polenta, mix together the topping ingredients and sprinkle on top. Bake for about 40 minutes until the top is browned and bubbling.

SERVES 6

# BAKED ROSEMARY POLENTA WITH A CRISP RED ONION TOPPING

A good warming, savoury, winter dish, using that most reliable of herbs, rosemary. My rosemary plants survive unscathed through all but the hardest winters, providing welcome aromatic flavour throughout the cold months. Rosemary needs a robust partner – it is quite assertive – but the red onions more than hold their own. If you can keep most of the onion slices intact, their concentric rings make the finished dish look especially attractive.

THE POLENTA BASE
230 g (8 oz) polenta or maize meal
270 ml (9 fl oz) cold water
500 ml (18 fl oz) hot water
1 level teaspoon salt
2 teaspoons finely chopped rosemary
15 g (½ oz) butter
110 g (4 oz) grated fresh Parmesan cheese
juice of half a lemon
freshly ground black pepper

FOR THE TOPPING
230 g (8 oz) red onions, sliced into wafer-thin rings
1 tablespoon olive oil, plus a little extra to oil the dish
1 teaspoon chopped rosemary
a pinch of sugar
salt and freshly ground black pepper

Oven temperature: 220°C (425°F, gas 7) – adjust for fan ovens

Cook the polenta as described in either of the two preceding recipes for about 15 minutes. Add the chopped rosemary and cook for another 5 minutes, then take the pan off the heat and stir in the butter, Parmesan and lemon juice. Taste, and add plenty of pepper and more salt if you think it needs it.

Pre-heat the oven if you haven't already done so.

Oil the largest baking dish or tray you possess, turn the polenta into it, and spread out as thinly as possible, to a depth of about 1 cm (½ inch). Don't worry if the edges are a bit rough. It may help to oil the palm of your hand and press down on the mixture. Score the surface with the back of a fork to make ridges. This is not purely for decoration, but also to increase the surface area which allows the top to get crisper. Bake uncovered for 20–30 minutes, until the top is brown and crisp.

Using your fingers, gently mix together all the topping ingredients (try not to break up the onion rings). Spread the topping evenly over the crisp polenta and return the dish to the oven for 10–15 minutes until the onions are brown and crisp.

SERVES 3

# AUBERGINES AND RED ONIONS ROASTED WITH MARSALA

Although rich in flavour, this dish is actually very low in fat, which makes it useful to have in the repertoire. It is nice served with a plain but carefully-cooked grain, such as quinoa or couscous; or it could even be used as a sauce for pasta. A good way of cooking quinoa is described on page 100.

Lemon thyme is an excellent and useful herb, not often available in the shops, but easy and trouble-free to grow. It stays green and palatable right through the winter, and makes such a neat little dome of foliage (especially when picked frequently) that it doesn't look out of place in a flower bed. It prefers a sunny spot and adapts happily to life in a pot or window box.

3 red onions, peeled and quartered
small bunch of fresh lemon thyme
2 medium aubergines
half a lemon, scrubbed and cut into about 8 chunks
1 tablespoon olive oil
salt
340 ml (12 fl oz) sweet Marsala

Oven temperature: 180°C (350°F, gas 4) – adjust for fan ovens

When quartering the onions, try to leave some of the root base-plate attached as this will help prevent them falling apart. Pick the leaves off the lemon thyme with as much fastidiousness as you can muster. It doesn't really matter if you leave some stems attached, but try and get rid of any particularly woody bits.

Cut the aubergine into chunks about the same size as the onion quarters. Put the prepared vegetables, lemon pieces and thyme into a large bowl, add the olive oil and give it a good swirl about so the oil is evenly distributed. Now add a little salt, pour on the Marsala and swirl again. You can leave it all to marinate for up to 2 hours at this stage, if you like, although this is not at all crucial.

Pre-heat the oven if you haven't already done so.

Place the marinaded vegetables and their liquid in a wide, shallow baking dish or tin, cover with foil and bake for 40 minutes. Remove the foil, give the dish a stir and bake uncovered for a further 10–15 minutes, until the vegetables are slightly browned and the cooking liquid has reduced to a few tablespoons of intense, syrupy sauce.

SERVES 2–3

# ROASTED CELERIAC WITH SHALLOTS, WALNUTS AND SOFT GOAT'S CHEESE

Cold-weather comfort food, this simple, savoury gratin needs only some good hot bread and a crisp salad such as *Garden leaf and herb salad with balsamic vinaigrette* (page 46) by way of accompaniment. Choose your goat's cheese carefully as they vary a good deal – it should be creamy and not too pungent. If you dislike goat's cheese, Mascarpone or cream cheese can be used instead.

2 medium-sized celeriac roots
4 large shallots, torpedo-shaped if you can get them
2 tablespoons olive oil
juice of a lemon
1 heaped teaspoon cumin seeds
salt and freshly ground black pepper
100 g (3½ oz) full fat soft goat's cheese
handful of roasted walnut pieces (see page 16 for roasting times)

Oven temperature: 200°C (400°F, gas 6) – adjust for fan ovens

Quickly peel the celeriac and cut into slices no more than 2 cm (1 inch) thick. Cut each slice in four, then put the chunks into water immediately to stop them going brown. Boil them in salted water for 5 minutes.

Peel the shallots and cut into 1 cm (½ inch) slices, then put them in a shallow roasting tin with the partly-cooked celeriac and the olive oil. Swirl them about with your fingers until the vegetables are evenly coated with oil, then add the lemon juice, cumin seeds, salt and pepper. Mix again, then cover the tin with foil and bake in the pre-heated oven for 40 minutes.

Remove the foil and bake for 10 minutes more. Dot spoonfuls of the cheese over the surface of the dish, turn up the oven to 220°C (425°F, gas 7) – adjust for fan ovens, and bake for another 7–10 minutes until the top is nicely browned. Scatter over the walnut pieces before serving.

SERVES 3

# PATTYPAN SQUASH FILLED WITH WALNUTS AND ROQUEFORT

This is a useful summer dinner party dish as it can be prepared ahead of time apart from the baking. Try serving it with some *Herb couscous* (page 103). Pattypans are those flat little squashes with scalloped sides, often sold as mini vegetables and available in both green and yellow. If you can't find them, this recipe can be made using courgettes, par-boiled, halved lengthways and scooped out to make boat shapes.

12 pattypan squash, 5–7 cm (2–3 inch) in diameter
1 large onion, peeled and finely chopped
1 tablespoon olive oil
15 g (½ oz) butter
2 cloves garlic, peeled and finely chopped
salt and freshly ground black pepper
60 g (2 oz) roasted walnuts, roughly chopped (see page 16 for roasting times)
100 g (3½ oz) Roquefort cheese, crumbled

Oven temperature: 200°C (400°F, gas 6) – adjust for fan ovens

Cut a biggish slice off the stalk end of the squashes, enough to be able to scoop them out for filling later. Also cut a small slice off the blossom ends, so they will sit without wobbling. Simmer them in salted water for 4 minutes, then drain and allow to cool until handleable.

Meanwhile fry the onion in the oil and butter until slightly brown and softened, adding the garlic for the last few minutes and seasoning with a little salt and pepper.

When the squash are cool enough to handle, scoop out cavities for the stuffing using a melon baller or small metal spoon. Season the cavities with salt and pepper, then share out the fried onion between them. Share out the walnut chunks next, reserving a few for later, then the crumbled cheese.

Bake uncovered in an oiled shallow tray in the pre-heated oven for about 20 minutes, until browned and bubbling. Put the reserved nuts on top about 5 minutes before the end of the cooking time – that way they won't burn.

SERVES 3

VARIATIONS

Substitute roasted pine kernels and Dolcelatte cheese for the walnuts and Roquefort.

This filling is also good with miniature winter squash such as *Jack be Little*, which can be prepared in the same way as pattypans. Cut a hole in the top and scoop out the seeds before stuffing.

# ROASTED BABY AUBERGINES WITH LEEKS AND MUSHROOMS

If you're lucky enough to find baby aubergines in the shops, or you grow them your-self, this is a nice way to eke them out – they are very expensive to buy and not very prolific growers!

4 large mushrooms, cleaned and quartered
6 small leeks, cleaned and trimmed into 5 cm (2 inch) lengths
250 g (9 oz) baby aubergines, cleaned and halved lengthwise,
    or left whole if very tiny
3 sprigs rosemary
6 sprigs lemon thyme
1 tablespoon olive oil
salt and freshly ground black pepper
220 ml (8 fl oz) dry white wine

Oven temperature: 220°C (425°F, gas 7) – adjust for fan ovens

If you're leaving the aubergines whole, prick them with a fork to avoid explosions. Place the vegetables and herbs in a bowl, pour on the oil and stir thoroughly until the vegetables are well coated. Season with salt and pepper, add the wine and stir to coat thoroughly. Leave them to marinade for at least 30 minutes, and anything up to several hours.

When you're ready to cook them, place the vegetables in a shallow roasting dish or tin. They should be in a single layer. Cover tightly with foil and cook in the pre-heated oven for about 30 minutes, until almost tender. If you use a ceramic dish they may take slightly longer to cook.

Remove the foil, baste the vegetables with the cooking liquid and then return the dish uncovered to the oven for about another 10 minutes, or until the vegetables are tender. Serve with pasta, garlic bread, rice or *Herb couscous* (page 103).

SERVES 2

# ROASTED MEDITERRANEAN VEGETABLES WITH HERBS AND GOAT'S CHEESE

This dish, a variation on the preceding recipe, is simplicity itself, and in relation to the minimal effort involved in its preparation, tastes disproportionately wonderful. The secret is in the freshness of the ingredients and the particular cheese used for the topping. Chêvre Blanc, the delicious French goat's cheese log with its powdery, ridged white rind, cooks beautifully – soft and melting below the surface, crisp and brown on top.

The goat's cheese log needs cutting into slices, which is difficult to do neatly unless you have a cheese wire. I usually ask them to slice it for me in the deli, and interleave it with grease-proof paper (otherwise it sticks together and is completely unmanageable), but if your cheese supplier is less obliging just slice it as best you can, or even crumble it, if necessary. The finished dish may look less glamorous but will taste just as good!

4 red onions, peeled and quartered
1 large aubergine, diced
1 large or 2 small red peppers, diced
3 sprigs fresh rosemary
small handful fresh lemon thyme (or ordinary culinary thyme)
2 tablespoons extra virgin olive oil
salt and freshly ground black pepper
small glass of dry wine, red or white (optional)
7–10 cm (3–4 inch) piece of Chêvre Blanc goat's cheese log, cut into 6 or 8 slices

Oven temperature: 200°C (400°F, gas 6) – adjust for fan ovens

When preparing the onions, try and leave some of the root base-plate intact, as it will prevent the quarters from disintegrating. Slice the aubergine into 1 cm (½ inch) rounds, then halve or quarter the rounds. The pepper should be cut into chunks of a similar size – big enough for each to make a decent mouthful.

Place the vegetables and herbs in a large, shallow roasting tin, pour on the oil and stir thoroughly. Season with salt and pepper. You might add a generous splash of dry wine at this stage, but it's by no means essential.

At this point, you can, if it's more convenient, cover and refrigerate for anything up to several hours before roasting.

Cover the tin tightly with foil and cook in the pre-heated oven for about 30 minutes.

Remove the foil, give the vegetables a stir and arrange the slices of cheese on top. Return the tin, uncovered, to the oven for about another 20–25 minutes, or until the cheese is brown and bubbling, and the vegetables tender.

Serve with baked potatoes, couscous, rice or pasta.

SERVES 2

# ONION AND MUSHROOM RAGOÛT WITH QUORN

In general I dislike meat substitutes – the very idea seems to imply a negative attitude towards vegetarian food, defining it in terms of a lack, rather than focusing on the wonderful ingredients vegetarians *can* use. The concept of a food trying so hard to be something other than itself seems to me both foolish and somehow dishonest. What's more, many of the meat substitutes available are decidedly second-rate in both flavour and texture. Anyone who is that desperate for meat should probably just carry on eating it.

Given my views on the subject, I was rather sniffy about Quorn when it was first introduced, but I had some at a friend's house and was instantly converted. Quorn chunks absorb flavours well, have a satisfyingly chewy texture, and don't disintegrate during cooking. I might not serve them at a dinner party but for everyday food they're very acceptable. I should perhaps point out that Quorn is not vegan – it contains egg white.

5 g (¼ oz) dried ceps or other wild mushrooms
500 g (1lb 2 oz) onions, preferably small pickling onions
1 tablespoon olive oil
15 g (½ oz) butter
230 g (8 oz) button mushrooms, cleaned and kept whole
1 small, finely chopped fresh red chilli pepper
2 cloves of garlic, peeled and chopped
170 g (6 oz) Quorn chunks
240 ml (8 fl oz) red wine
juice of 1 lemon
salt and freshly ground black pepper
1 level tablespoon Dijon mustard
3 pinches of sugar
1 tablespoon shoyu or other natural soy sauce
2 tablespoons of chopped parsley

Put the dried mushrooms in a small jug and pour on enough boiling water just to cover them – about 90 ml (3 fl oz). Leave them to soak for at least 20 minutes, then pour the soaking water through a fine sieve into another jug.

Rinse the soaked mushrooms under running water, just in case they contained any debris, then chop them roughly.

Peel the onions. To loosen the skins blanch them in boiling water for 2–3 minutes then drain. If you have small onions leave them whole, otherwise quarter them, trying to leave some of the base attached so they stay together during cooking.

Heat the oil and butter in a wide, heavy pan and sauté the onions over a moderate heat for about 10 minutes until they are slightly browned.

Add both the dried and fresh mushrooms, the chilli, garlic and Quorn, and sauté for a few minutes more.

Pour in the wine, mushroom-soaking liquid and lemon juice, add a little salt, then simmer uncovered for about 30 minutes, stirring occasionally, until the vegetables are tender.

The liquid should be greatly reduced in volume, but if the pan looks to be drying out too much during cooking, add a little water as necessary.

Finally, stir in the mustard, sugar, shoyu, pepper and most of the parsley. Taste, add more salt and pepper if necessary, and garnish with the remaining parsley.

Serve with rice, couscous or a potato dish such as *Potato gratin with garlic and rosemary* (page 136).

SERVES 2–3

# EGG AND SPINACH PIZZA

A truly splendid pizza, this. My absolute favourite pizza topping, ever. It should be made with fresh, not frozen, spinach and the biggest, freshest organic free-range eggs you can find.

Fast action dried yeast (see ingredients) is the type you mix directly with the flour. It generally comes in small sachets and is not the same as ordinary dried yeast, which has to be dissolved in liquid before mixing.

## PIZZA DOUGH

310 g (11 oz) strong white bread flour
½ level tablespoon sugar
½ level teaspoon salt
½ level teaspoon fast action dried yeast
2 tablespoons olive oil, plus a little extra
150 ml (5 fl oz) water, lukewarm

## PIZZA TOPPING

230 g (8 oz) fresh spinach, washed and trimmed
30 g (1 oz) butter
2 or 3 cloves of garlic, peeled and crushed
salt and freshly ground black pepper
90 g (3 oz) sun-dried tomato paste
3 or 4 fresh, ripe tomatoes, thinly sliced
2 large eggs
30 g (1 oz) freshly grated Parmesan cheese
200 g (7 oz) Mozzarella cheese
12 black Kalamata olives, stoned

Oven temperature: 220°C (425°F, gas 7) – adjust for fan ovens

First make the pizza dough. Put all the dry ingredients, including the yeast, in a bowl and mix thoroughly. Stir in the oil and water, then knead the dough. You may need to add a little extra water – flours vary greatly in their capacity to absorb liquid. Turn the dough out onto a clean, floured work surface and knead thoroughly by hand for about 10 minutes, until it is smooth and elastic. If you have a food processor or heavy-duty food mixer with a dough attachment, by all means use it instead.

## HOW TO KNEAD DOUGH

Gather the dough together with your hands, straighten your arms and press the dough down and slightly away from yourself with the heels of your hands, using the full weight of your body (if your work surface is too high for this to be feasible, stand on something to make yourself a bit taller). Flatten the dough with the heel of your hand, fold it over roughly in half and press down again. Give the squashed dough about a quarter turn, fold in half, press down again, leaning your body weight into the push. Keep repeating the rhythmic turning, folding and pressing – that's all there is to it. If the dough sticks to the work surface just sprinkle on a little extra flour.

Oil a clean bowl with a little olive oil, put the kneaded dough into it and flip it over so that all its surface is thinly coated with oil. Cover the bowl with a clean, damp tea towel (or cling-film) and place it in a warm, draught-free place (such as an airing cupboard) to rise until it has doubled in size. This takes anything from thirty to ninety minutes, depending on the temperature. However long it seems to be taking, don't be tempted to cut short the process. It's important the yeast is properly active and the dough lively.

Tip the dough back out onto a floured surface, punch it down, knead it again for a moment or two, then cut in half. Shape each half into a ball and roll out two pizza bases, approximately 25 cm (10 inches) in diameter. Transfer them onto large, oiled baking sheets or pizza trays (roll them round a rolling pin to lift without tearing), cover with a damp tea-towel and put them back in the warm to rise again. The second rising should take less time than the first, but don't be tempted to apply the pizza topping until you can see the dough has risen.

## MAKE THE TOPPING

Dry the washed spinach in a salad-spinner or clean tea-towel, then melt the butter in a large saucepan. Add the crushed garlic and spinach, and cook briefly just until the spinach has wilted, stirring constantly. Add salt and pepper to taste, and set the pan aside to cool slightly.

Pre-heat the oven if you have not already done so.

Dilute the sun-dried tomato paste with a little boiling water to get a spreadable consistency, then spread it over the pizza bases. Arrange the sliced tomatoes in a single layer on top and season well with salt and pepper.

About 5 cm (2 inches) in from the edge of each pizza, make a circle of cooked spinach on top of the tomato layer, leaving an egg-sized space in the centre, and making sure that some of the tomato layer is showing around the edge. Mound up the spinach into a slight ridge, volcano-fashion, to contain the egg.

Break an egg onto the centre of each pizza, then sprinkle grated Parmesan cheese over the surface of the egg and the spinach. Arrange slices of Mozzarella cheese around the outside edge of the pizza, overlapping the spinach and tomato layers but leaving the egg yolk visible. Finally, tuck the olives between the cheese slices.

Bake in the hot oven for 15–20 minutes until the egg is set and the cheese brown and bubbling. Serve with plenty of freshly ground black pepper.

MAKES 2 PIZZAS

# CALZONE FILLED WITH CAVOLO NERO, SUN-DRIED TOMATOES AND HERBS

Calzone are just great big hefty folded pizza pasties! Nothing refined about them, but they make wonderful food for the famished. Usually served hot, they are also very nice cold, and make good picnic food – the robust flavours stand up well to outdoor dining.

THE DOUGH

1 recipe pizza dough, see page 116

THE FILLING

1 medium-sized onion, peeled and chopped
½ teaspoon dried *herbes de Provence*
1 tablespoon olive oil
2 cloves of garlic, finely chopped
salt and freshly ground black pepper
200 g (7 oz) Cavolo Nero black kale (or Savoy cabbage), de-stalked and shredded
90 g (3 oz) diced Gorgonzola cheese
3 sun-dried tomato halves, preserved in oil, drained and chopped
2 rounded tablespoons sun-dried tomato paste
1 fresh tomato, diced
30 g (1 oz) of freshly grated Parmesan cheese
4 black olives, stoned and halved

Oven temperature: 200°C (400°F, gas 6) – adjust for fan ovens

Make the dough exactly as described on page 116 and leave it to rise.

MAKE THE FILLING

In a large pan, sauté the onion and dried herbs in the olive oil over a medium heat for about 10 minutes, until slightly softened.

Add the garlic, a little salt and the washed, shredded kale, with any water that still adheres to it, and stir well for a few minutes longer until it is hot.

Put a lid on the pan, turn the heat down to low and cook gently for a further 10 minutes or so, until the kale is quite tender but still has a little bite (to allow for it cooking a bit more in the oven).

Take the pan off the heat, let it cool, then stir in all the remaining ingredients. Add a generous grind of pepper, taste, and add extra salt if needed.

## ASSEMBLE THE CALZONE

Pre-heat the oven now, if you haven't already done so.

After the first rising, punch down the dough, cut it in half and roll out two 25 cm (10 inch) circles of dough, as described for the pizza in the preceding recipe. Cover the dough with a clean damp tea towel and leave it to rise in a warm place, until doubled in thickness.

Lift each circle of dough onto the oiled baking sheet or pizza tray you intend to use for baking, before filling the calzone (when filled they are tricky to move).

Divide the calzone filling between each circle, spreading it in a semi-circle over half of each piece of dough, but leaving a 3 cm (1 inch) margin of dough around the edge clear for sealing. Moisten the edge of each circle with water, and fold them in half to make large semi-circular pasties. Pinch the dough firmly to seal, and stab a vent hole in each one to allow steam to escape. Brush them with a little olive oil for a nice finish.

Bake in the pre-heated oven for 20–30 minutes, until golden brown. When the calzone are almost cooked, carefully remove them from the tray and put them directly on the oven shelf for the last few minutes of cooking to make sure the bases are crisp. The filling will be extremely hot when the pasties first emerge from the oven, so leave them to cool for a short while before serving. For children especially, you might want to cut them open to allow some of the steam to escape.

MAKES 2 LARGE CALZONE

# BUCKWHEAT PANCAKES FILLED WITH SPINACH AND SUN-DRIED TOMATOES

This is quite a nice dinner party main course. People always seem to like pancakes, perhaps because of their festive connotations. Both filling and pancakes can be made anything up to two days ahead of time and refrigerated, but the dish should only be assembled immediately before baking. Fresh spinach is crucial; frozen spinach is far too watery.

THE PANCAKES

90 g (3 oz) buckwheat flour
130 g (4½ oz) white flour
½ level teaspoon salt
3 eggs
230 ml (8 fl oz) milk
230 ml (8 fl oz) water
a little butter for cooking

THE FILLING

500 g (1 lb 2 oz) spinach, washed, shredded and dried
15 g (½ oz) butter
1 tablespoon olive oil
1 small onion, peeled and chopped
2 cloves of garlic, finely sliced
1 red chilli, finely chopped (more or less, as preferred)
grated rind from one lemon
salt and freshly ground black pepper
10 oil-preserved sun-dried tomato halves, sliced
3 or 4 tablespoons sun-dried tomato paste
1 or 2 egg whites (optional)

THE TOPPING

either half quantity of *Cheese sauce* (page 185),
    or 5 tablespoons of double cream plus a little freshly grated Parmesan cheese
finely sliced chives or spring onion greens to garnish

Oven temperature: 180°C (350°F, gas 4) – adjust for fan ovens

THE PANCAKES

If you have a food processor, put in the ingredients in the order listed and whiz everything together for a few seconds, scraping down the sides of the bowl with a spatula as necessary, until the batter is smooth.

To make the batter by hand, use a wire balloon whisk or a fork. Place the dry ingredients in a mixing bowl and stir them together. In a large jug whisk together the eggs, water and milk for just a few moments to amalgamate them. Make a well in the centre of the flour and start to add the liquid gradually, whisking. The flour will fall in towards the centre and gradually be mixed in. Whenever the mixture starts to feel too stiff to whisk easily, just add a little more liquid, always into the centre of the bowl. Continue until the liquid is all incorporated and the batter is free of lumps.

Whichever method you use, let the batter sit in a cool place for at least 30 minutes before attempting to cook the pancakes. Before starting to cook, give the batter a stir and, if it has gone very thick, add a little more milk or water.

I usually cook the pancakes in a 20 cm (8 inch) frying pan, but the exact size is not very important. Heat a small piece of butter in the pancake pan for a few moments over a moderate heat, swirling it around to make sure the base of the pan is evenly coated as the butter melts.

Pour in enough batter just to cover the base of the pan. Tilt the pan around to spread out the batter thinly. Let the batter set for a few moments, until the surface starts to look slightly dry, then loosen around the edge with a knife and turn the pancake over. Shake the pan a little, then toss if you're adventurous; otherwise use a thin spatula. Both sides should end up lightly browned.

If you want to use them later, cool the pancakes on a wire rack before stacking them up and wrapping them in plastic. If you don't cool them they have a tendency to stick together, which is a pain. If you're ultra cautious or intend to freeze them, interleave them with silicon paper.

The first pancake is often a bit of a disaster (bin it if need be), but once the pan is thoroughly heated and seasoned, subsequent ones are usually OK. The pan may gradually over-heat, in which case waft it to and fro between pancakes and turn the heat down very slightly. You will only need to add tiny amounts of butter to the pan between pancakes. Once you get into a rhythm, production is quite speedy and very satisfying.

THE FILLING

Make sure the prepared spinach is thoroughly dried before you cook it, as the filling should be dry enough to prevent the pancakes going soggy. A salad spinner or shaker is probably the easiest method of dealing with it.

Warm the butter and olive oil in a large pan over a medium heat. Sauté the onion for about 15 minutes, stirring occasionally until it begins to soften. Add the garlic, chilli and lemon rind. Stir to un-clog the lemon rind, then add the spinach and stir again. Add about half a teaspoon of salt. Cook, stirring, over quite a high heat, for about 5 minutes until the spinach is wilted but not completely soggy. The cooking time will vary according to the spinach used, but you should aim to leave it slightly undercooked, as it will be cooked again after the pancakes are filled.

If you plan to add the optional egg whites, it is worth cooling the pan before you do so to prevent them congealing, particularly if you have used a pan with a heavy base which retains the heat.

Take the pan off the heat and stir in the sun-dried tomato slices and puree, followed by the egg whites if you're using them. They will make the filling firmer, but are really only worth bothering with if you happen to have some left over from a recipe using just yolks. Add freshly ground black pepper, and extra salt if necessary.

PUTTING IT TOGETHER

Place a couple of tablespoons of filling on each pancake, spread it into a sausage shape and roll the pancake around it. Pack the filled pancakes closely in an oiled rectangular baking dish, pour over the cheese sauce or cream. If using cream, sprinkle a little grated Parmesan cheese on top. Bake in the pre-heated oven for about 20 minutes, until the top is browned and bubbling. Garnish with a light sprinkle of chive rings just before serving.

If you possess any individual gratin dishes of a suitable size and shape, by all means use them. They look nice and eliminate the risk of accidents during serving.

SERVES 4

# COURGETTE RIBBON NOODLES

Vegetable 'pasta' without the stodge – a concept of quite brilliant simplicity. The courgettes are sliced lengthways into long thin strips, lightly steamed until they flop like noodles, served with any of the sauces suitable for pasta, and topped with fresh grated Parmesan cheese. Cooked in this very simple way, they retain their distinct character and flavour.

I first encountered the idea in a restaurant, the name and location of which I have since completely forgotten, so if the inspired individual who dreamt it up happens to read this, please accept my sincere apologies for the lack of acknowledgement, and get in touch with me for a mention in any future editions of this book.

I like to use a mixture of green and yellow courgettes, but either alone would be fine. Whatever kind you use, try to get them quite evenly matched in size. As to the sauce, any of the more creamy pasta sauces marry well with courgette noodles, but unless you want an exceptionally low fat meal, avoid anything too watery – a couple of suggestions are given below. As with flour-based pasta, don't overdo the sauce – the courgettes should be lightly coated, not swimming.

### 230 g (8 oz) courgettes per person

Wash the courgettes, dry, and top and tail them. Slice them lengthwise into 3mm (1/8 inch) ribbons (about the thickness of a pound coin). Most food processors have an attachment that does this very quickly.

Have the sauce, grated cheese and anything else you plan to serve with the dish ready and waiting, since the courgettes take only a couple of minutes to cook.

Salt the courgettes lightly and cook them in a large steamer for 2–3 minutes over fast boiling water, until just tender. They should still have some bite but be soft enough to bend, so they actually behave like pasta. Remove the steamer basket from over the hot water and let the courgettes sit in a warm airy place for a couple of minutes so that some of the steam dissipates, then stir them gently into the waiting hot sauce and serve in warmed bowls, topped with the grated Parmesan cheese.

Serve with *Summer tomato sauce with basil and cream* (page 193), and stir in some finely-shredded fresh basil just before serving. This look very pretty when a mixture of yellow and green-skinned courgettes are used. If you feel the need for carbohydrates, serve hot garlic bread on the side.

*Garlic mushroom sauce* (page 188) is another good accompaniment and is nice topped with a sprinkling of roasted walnut pieces.

# SAUTÉ OF MIXED SUMMER SQUASH

This is a lovely way of using really choice home-grown courgettes, picked at finger thickness – much smaller than you generally find them in the shops, but it is still good when made with larger courgettes if these are all you can get.

Yellow courgettes seem to bruise more easily than green ones, so virtually the only way to get them in prime condition is to grow your own and handle them gently. It's worth the effort as they are so delicious and decorative. They are also much easier to spot amongst the forests of green foliage, and hence less likely to turn into marrows through oversight!

The pattypans are both easy to grow and prolific – just one plant would probably provide more than enough for an average household.

450 g (1 lb) mixed green and yellow courgettes, evenly sliced
230 g (8 oz) small pattypan squash, sliced to the same thickness as the
    courgettes, giving some scalloped pieces
1 tablespoon olive oil
15 g (½ oz) butter
2 cloves of garlic, peeled and crushed
salt and freshly ground black pepper
30 g (1 oz) roasted pine kernels
a little fresh Parmesan cheese, shaved into slivers with a potato peeler

Sauté the courgettes and squash in the olive oil and butter, quite briskly, so they brown without going soggy. When they are nearly cooked, which might be as little as 2–3 minutes if they are tiny and fresh, stir in the crushed garlic and cook a couple of minutes longer. Season with salt and pepper, stir in the pine kernels and serve with *Herb couscous* (page 103), to which a few shredded basil leaves have been added in the final stages of cooking. Top with the shaved Parmesan.

SERVES 2–3

# TOMATO AND PEPPER RAGOÛT WITH GRILLED GOAT'S CHEESE

Make this dish in late summer when ripe tomatoes are plentiful. It can be truly delicious given first-rate ingredients, so taste your tomatoes and reject any that are not bursting with flavour. If you can also get your hands on some long, thin Hungarian or Moroccan red peppers – the type with a distinct paprika flavour – then you'll be in vegetable heaven.

1 tablespoon olive oil
15 g (½ oz) butter
2 teaspoons ground paprika (optional)
2 large or 3 small onions, coarsely chopped
2 or 3 red peppers, de-seeded and cut into large chunks
salt and freshly ground black pepper
6–8 large ripe tomatoes, peeled and coarsely chopped
6 garlic cloves, peeled but left whole
1 small potato, peeled and grated
up to 1 tablespoon balsamic vinegar
170 g (6 oz) Chèvre Blanc goat's cheese log

Heat the oil and butter in a wide, heavy frying pan, and add the paprika if you are using it. If I have really good peppers I tend to leave it out, but if ordinary bell peppers are all I can get, I think it's worth adding. Fry for a couple of minutes, then add the onions and peppers. Cook over a moderate heat for about 10 minutes, stirring frequently.

Add about a teaspoon of salt, then stir in the tomatoes, garlic and grated potato. Simmer gently with the pan uncovered for about 40 minutes, stirring occasionally, until everything is tender. If the vegetables seem to be catching, add a little water (or a slosh of white wine!), as necessary. Most of the liquid should be allowed to evaporate – the dish should not be watery.

When the vegetables are cooked, stir in some freshly ground black pepper, check the seasoning and add more salt if necessary. Stir in a little balsamic vinegar, tasting as you go. At this point, if your tomatoes were less than perfectly ripe, you may like to add a pinch or two of sugar, but don't overdo it.

Arrange slices of goat's cheese over the surface of the ragoût and place the pan under a hot grill, as near the heat source as you can get it, until the cheese is brown and bubbling.

Serve with baked potatoes, hot garlic bread, rice or other grains. It's actually very good served inside a giant Yorkshire pudding.

SERVES 2

VARIATION
Substitute big dollops of cream cheese, Mascarpone or even slices of Mozarella for the goat's cheese.

# THAI GREEN CURRY

This is a beautiful vegan dish – aromatic and colourful.

⅓ quantity *Thai green curry paste* (page 207)
2 onions, peeled and chopped
1 tablespoon groundnut (peanut) oil
4 cloves of garlic, peeled and finely chopped
about 1 kg (2 lb) assorted vegetables (see below for suggested combinations)
4 Kaffir lime leaves, left whole
1 level teaspoon palm sugar (optional)
400 ml (14 fl oz) can coconut milk
salt and freshly ground black pepper
juice of half a lime (or more, to taste)
generous handful of fresh coriander leaves, washed, dried and coarsely chopped
a few Thai basil leaves, washed, dried and coarsely chopped
handful of marinaded tofu chunks, roasted cashews or roasted almonds to garnish

Fry the green curry paste with the chopped onions in the oil, until the onions have started to soften. Add the garlic and whatever vegetables you have chosen for the curry (see suggestions below), plus the lime leaves, palm sugar, salt and pepper, and fry a bit longer.

Gradually stir in the coconut milk, and simmer until vegetables are tender. Approximate timings are given for the different combinations below, but these are for guidance only – test frequently.

When the vegetables are cooked, taste, adjust the seasonings and add the lime juice. Stir in the fresh coriander, basil leaves and roasted nuts or tofu chunks just before serving. Serve with Thai fragrant rice, jasmine rice or noodles.

SERVES 4

SUGGESTED VEGETABLE COMBINATIONS

Don't be tempted to add too many different vegetable ingredients – you only need two or three distinct flavours and textures.

- Baby sweetcorn (halved lengthwise), French beans or baby runner beans, red peppers (20–30 minutes).
- Quorn chunks, cauliflower and carrots (40–50 minutes). Note: Quorn contains egg white, so is not vegan.
- Courgettes, yellow peppers, halved cherry tomatoes (20–40 minutes, depending on the age and size of the courgettes).

# WINTER VEGETABLE STEW

Hot, savoury comfort food this – a simple, warming, old-fashioned stew of winter root vegetables. If you enjoyed beef stew and dumplings in pre-vegetarian days, this should appeal. The dried soup mix is available just about everywhere, but scan the list of ingredients to make sure there's nothing that needs pre-soaking, or that takes an inordinate amount of time to cook – whole haricot beans or marrowfat peas are sometimes included and can cause problems. Note that salt is not added until the end of the cooking time, as it can prevent the pulses in the dried soup mix getting tender.

2 tablespoons olive oil
3 large onions, peeled and chopped
4 cloves of garlic, peeled and chopped
4 large carrots, peeled and diced
1 large parsnip, peeled and diced
1 small swede, peeled and diced
2 or 3 potatoes, peeled and diced
3 or 4 stalks of celery, sliced
handful of dried soup mix (barley, split peas, lentils, etc.)
400 g (14 oz) can of chopped tomatoes
about 570 ml (1 pint) well-flavoured vegetable stock
60 g (2 oz) creamed coconut, chopped (optional)
salt and freshly ground black pepper

Warm the olive oil in a large soup pan and add the prepared vegetables. Sauté, stirring, for about 10 minutes, then add the dried soup mix and the canned tomatoes with their juice. Top up with enough vegetable stock just to cover the vegetables. Cover the pan and simmer gently for 30–40 minutes, stirring occasionally, until all the soup mix components are tender. The exact time will depend on the composition of your dried soup mix.

If you want a creamy stew, add the creamed coconut at the end of the cooking time. This amount is enough to give a creamy texture, but not enough to give a strong flavour of coconut. Add salt and pepper to taste and serve with hot garlic bread.

SERVES 4

VARIATION
Add *Plain or herb dumplings* (page 43) for the last 25 minutes of cooking time.

# VEGETABLE
# ACCOMPANIMENTS
# AND SIDE DISHES

*In this chapter you will find a selection of vegetable side dishes to accompany main courses. Some are substantial enough to form the basis of a meal in their own right, perhaps with a little padding. All are meant to be served hot, and most feature winter vegetables, hence they are more suited to the colder months.*

# JERUSALEM ARTICHOKE AND RED ONION SAUTÉ

This savoury, low-fat winter sauté makes a good accompaniment to egg dishes such as soufflés and frittatas. If you're serving it with a soufflé, make sure it's cooked a few minutes before the soufflé is ready. The sauté can be kept warm quite easily, but the soufflé must be served immediately, before it deflates.

4 small red onions
7 g (¼ oz) butter (vegans substitute extra olive oil)
1 tablespoon olive oil
piece of fresh ginger about half the size of your thumb, peeled and finely chopped
2 teaspoons fennel seeds
450g (1 lb) Jerusalem artichokes, peeled and sliced into 5 mm (¼ inch) rounds
3 or 4 tablespoons vegetable stock or water
salt and freshly ground black pepper

Peel the onions and cut them into quarters lengthwise, leaving enough of the base to keep them connected. In a wide shallow pan, melt the butter, along with the olive oil, over a medium heat and sauté the onion quarters, ginger and fennel seeds. After about 7 minutes add the artichoke slices and continue cooking over a moderate to high heat for a few minutes more until the vegetables are slightly browned.

At this point add 3–4 tablespoons of hot water or vegetable stock and about half a teaspoon of salt, bring it up to the boil, put a lid on the pan and reduce the heat to a gentle simmer. Cook, shaking the pan occasionally for about 25 minutes until the vegetables are tender but not disintegrating. Have a look occasionally to make sure all is well – you may need to add a little extra liquid to the pan if it seems in danger of drying out.

When the artichokes are tender remove the lid and, if there is much cooking liquid left, turn up the heat for a minute or two until it has more or less evaporated. Taste, and adjust the seasoning.

Note: I have sometimes found that not all the artichokes cook at the same rate, so I suggest you test a few to make sure all are cooked.

## VARIATION

This dish is fine as an accompaniment just as it is, but to pad it out into a main meal for two, simply add a little cubed or crumbled cheese just before serving. A good mature Cheddar works well, likewise Stilton.

SERVES 4 AS A SIDE DISH

# CELERIAC GRATIN WITH INDIAN SPICES

Like the preceding recipe, this gratin makes a good winter accompaniment to egg dishes. The same comment about timing also applies.

1 large or 2 small celeriac roots, peeled and diced
a few drops of lemon juice
2 tablespoons olive oil
1 large onion, peeled and chopped
2 teaspoons fennel seeds
½ level teaspoon asafoetida (an Indian spice)
2 level teaspoons garam masala
salt and freshly ground black pepper

Oven temperature: 200°C (400°F, gas 6) – adjust for fan ovens

As you peel the celeriac drop it straight into acidulated water (water to which a little lemon juice has been added) to prevent it from browning. Boil a large pan of salted water, then drain the celeriac cubes and add to the pan. Simmer for 8–10 minutes until they are tender.

While the celeriac is cooking, heat the oil in a shallow pan and sauté the onion, fennel seeds and asafoetida briskly, stirring from time to time. When the onions are slightly browned take the pan off the heat and stir in the garam masala.

Add the drained, cooked celeriac to the pan and stir well, so it gets evenly coated with the oil, onions and spices.

Season with salt and pepper, then place on a baking tray in a single layer. Bake uncovered in the pre-heated oven for 10–12 minutes until brown and crisp.

SERVES 3

# CELERIAC MASH WITH POTATOES, CELERY AND LOVAGE

If serving two or more hot dishes together, it is as well to choose only one where the timing is critical – this delicious wintery mash, flecked with green celery and lovage leaves, can sit happily in the oven for up to half an hour without spoiling.

1 kg (2 lb) celeriac
a few drops of lemon juice
1 kg (2 lb) floury potatoes
5 or 6 stalks of celery
salt and freshly ground black pepper
about 15 g (½ oz) butter (vegans substitute olive oil)
2 tablespoons finely chopped lovage or celery leaves

Peel the celeriac and cut it into chunks, dropping them straight into acidulated water (water to which a few drops of lemon juice has been added) to prevent them from browning. Peel the potatoes and cut them into chunks about the same size as the celeriac. Chop the celery quite finely.

Boil all the vegetables in sufficient salted water just to barely cover the vegetables for about 20 minutes until tender.

Drain, but save the cooking water, which will be a well-flavoured stock suitable for soup or risotto-making.

Mash the vegetables with a potato masher as thoroughly as you can manage, adding some butter and finely chopped lovage or celery leaves. Don't be tempted to put it in the food processor, as it will turn to nasty slime.

If the mash is too solid, thin with some of the cooking water, cream or milk, as you prefer. Taste, and add extra seasoning if needed.

The mash can either be served immediately just as it is, or placed in an oven-proof dish and baked for a time to brown the top. Run a fork through the top of the mash before baking to get crispy brown ridges.

SERVES 6

# BRAISED CHICORY WITH SHALLOTS, MUSTARD AND DILL

Another nice wintery vegetable dish, this chicory goes well with *Sweet-potato pie with Puy lentils in a wine sauce* (page: 88). It could also be served alone as a starter, with some hot bread to mop up the pan juices.

15 g (½ oz) butter
170 g (6 oz) small shallots, peeled but left whole
230 g (8 oz) chicory, halved lengthwise
½ tablespoon mild mustard (smooth or grainy, as you prefer)
2 pinches sugar
170 ml (6 fl oz) vegetable stock
a splash of cream (optional)
grated nutmeg
3 tablespoons grated fresh Parmesan cheese
2 tablespoons chopped fresh dill

Use a wide, shallow, frying pan with a well-fitting lid for this dish. Melt the butter over a medium heat and swirl the shallots around in it for a few minutes until they start to colour. Add the chicory and allow it to brown slightly, particularly on the cut side.

Mix the mustard and sugar with the stock, pour onto the vegetables and bring it all to the boil. Depending on how salty the stock is, you may need to add salt at this point. Reduce the heat, cover the pan and simmer until the vegetables are tender – about 15 minutes.

If there is much liquid left over you may need to reduce it slightly. Turn up the heat and boil, uncovered, until only about 4 tablespoons remain. Stir in the cream, if using it, and add a little grated nutmeg.

Take the pan off the heat, sprinkle on the cheese, and put the lid back on for a couple of minutes until the cheese has melted. Garnish with chopped dill and serve.

SERVES 3

# CLAY-BAKED NEW POTATOES WITH GARLIC AND HERBS

This dish is incredibly simple and easy to make, but tastes wonderful. It would qualify as one of those useful dishes you can bung in the oven and forget about until it's ready, apart from needing a quick stir half-way through the cooking time. It is also entirely fat-free, but doesn't taste in the least like diet food, and is lovely when you want something soothing and flavoursome, but not too rich. Don't be tempted to add butter or any other fat – I've tried it and it's better without.

If you have a fan oven switch off the fan if you can, otherwise reduce the temperature slightly or the dish tends to dry out. If you don't have a lidded earthenware casserole, I suggest you cook this in a loose parcel of foil. Cast iron casseroles get too hot; oven-proof glassware doesn't conduct the heat well enough.

about 500 g (1 lb 2 oz) small new potatoes, scrubbed and left whole
6–8 cloves of garlic, peeled and left whole
generous pinch or two of dried *herbes de Provence*
salt and freshly ground black pepper
3 tablespoons of water

Oven temperature: 200°C (400°F, gas 6) – adjust for fan ovens

Try to make this dish with tiny new potatoes, but if you can only get larger ones then cut them into chunks of a uniform size – about 2–3 cm (1 inch). Put the potatoes, peeled garlic, herbs, salt and pepper into a deep, glazed earthenware casserole for which you have a lid. Pour in the water and swirl everything about using your hand or a large spoon. Put the lid on and bake in the pre-heated oven for 50–60 minutes. Half-way through the cooking time give the pot a stir. That's all!

I usually serve this topped with a generous portion of organic cottage cheese or sour cream, accompanied by a crisp leafy salad, and call it dinner.

SERVES 2 FOR DINNER, 4 AS AN ACCOMPANIMENT

# MASHED POTATOES WITH PESTO, PARMESAN AND PINE KERNELS

Comfort food *par excellence*, and a great way of using up leftover mashed potatoes. With a generous serving of oven-roasted peppers on the side, and a bottle of robust red wine, this makes a satisfying cold-weather dinner.

60 g (2 oz) pesto (bought is fine for this)
60 g (2 oz) Parmesan cheese, freshly grated
600 g (1 lb 5 oz) mashed potatoes
milk to mix
15 g (½ oz) fresh basil, finely chopped
salt and freshly ground black pepper
20 g (¾ oz) pine kernels

Oven temperature: 200°C (400°F, gas 6) – adjust for fan ovens

Beat the pesto and about half the Parmesan cheese into the mashed potato using a wooden spoon or a hand-held electric mixer. Don't use a food processor or the potatoes will subside into a revolting glutinous mess. If the mixture seems too stiff, thin it with a few tablespoons of milk.

Stir in the chopped basil, season to taste with salt and pepper, then spread the mixture into a wide, shallow oven-proof dish. Go over the surface with the back of a fork to decorate, if you feel inclined. Sprinkle the remaining cheese and pine kernels over the surface.

Bake in the pre-heated oven for 15–20 minutes until the top is brown and crisp, and the potatoes are heated through. The exact oven temperature doesn't really matter – vary it according to what else you're cooking, but keep an eye on the pine kernels as they burn easily.

SERVES 4–6 AS A SIDE DISH

# POTATO GRATIN WITH GARLIC AND ROSEMARY

This dish requires small waxy salad potatoes such as *Charlotte*, which have a good flavour and hold their shape without disintegrating. It is very simple to make, quite delicious and mercifully low in fat.

You will need a wide (30–40 cm, 12–14 inch) shallow oven-proof dish to bake it in.

450 g (1 lb) small salad potatoes
15 g (½ oz) butter (vegans substitute olive oil)
280 ml (10 fl oz) vegetable stock
2 small onions, peeled and thinly sliced
2 cloves of garlic, peeled and thinly sliced
3 or 4 small sprigs of fresh rosemary
salt and freshly ground black pepper

Oven temperature: 180°C (350°F, gas 4) – adjust for fan ovens

Wash the potatoes and slice them into discs, no more than 4 mm (⅕ inch) thick. Heat the vegetable stock to just below boiling point. Use some of the butter to oil the baking dish, and dissolve the remainder in the hot vegetable stock.

Put the sliced potatoes, onions, garlic and rosemary into the baking dish and mix them together using your hands. Season with salt and pepper and pour over the hot vegetable stock. Cover the dish, either with a lid or foil, and bake for 30 minutes. Remove the lid and bake for another 30 minutes, 1 hour in total. The top should be slightly brown and crisp at this point, and most of the liquid evaporated.

SERVES 3

# RED ONIONS WITH SEVILLE ORANGE AND MARSALA

This invigorating winter dish combines the intense flavours of bitter orange and sweet Marsala wine with melting, slow-cooked chunks of red onion. Seville oranges are only available for a short time during January and early February each year, but they freeze well, if you decide you can't live without them. Alternatively, they can simply be omitted. The character of the finished dish will be radically altered, but is still very good. Interesting enough to stand alone as a starter, accompanied only by a chunk of good bread, this dish also makes a lovely sauce for pasta, baked potatoes or a nut roast.

750 g (1 lb 10 oz) red onions, evenly matched in size
30g (1 oz) butter (vegans substitute olive oil)
150 ml (5 fl oz) sweet Marsala wine
grated rind and juice of 2 Seville oranges
1 level teaspoon salt
3 sprigs rosemary

Peel the onions, leaving as much of the base attached as possible to prevent them disintegrating during cooking, and halve them lengthwise. Melt the butter in a large (30 cm, 12 inch), heavy frying pan, and fry the onions, cut side down, over a moderate heat until well-browned, shaking the pan occasionally to prevent the onions from sticking. The onions should fit into the pan in a single layer.

Turn them over, so that the browned, cut sides are uppermost. Add the Marsala, orange juice and rind, salt, rosemary, and enough water to come half-way up the onions. Bring the onions to the boil, turn the heat down to a slow simmer, cover the pan, and cook slowly for 30–35 minutes, until the onions are meltingly tender.

Remove the pan lid and turn up the heat for a few minutes to reduce the cooking liquid to a few tablespoons of intense, syrupy sauce.

SERVES 4

# SPICED RED CABBAGE WITH MARSALA AND APPLES

This lovely winter cabbage dish has a vaguely medieval aura, with its rich, purple colouring and intense mix of sweet and savoury flavours. Good with *Terrine of cashews, almonds and apples* (page 90), it would also go well with roasted root vegetables, stuffed mushrooms, mashed potatoes, omelettes or soufflées. It improves with keeping so make it the day before you want to eat it, if possible. It can be re-heated in a foil-covered dish in the oven.

2 tablespoons olive oil
3 onions, quartered and thinly sliced
1 thumb-sized piece of fresh ginger, peeled and thinly sliced
3 cloves of garlic, peeled and thinly sliced
1 fresh red chilli, de-seeded and finely chopped
1 medium-sized red cabbage, finely shredded
1 level teaspoon of salt
180 ml (6 fl oz) sweet Marsala wine
2 apples, preferably Cox's Orange Pippins, peeled and diced

Warm the oil in a large, heavy pan and fry the onions over a gentle heat for a few minutes. Add the ginger, garlic and chilli and stir them for a moment or two, then stir in the cabbage. When it has heated through, add the salt and Marsala, bring it to the boil, then put on a lid and turn the heat down to a simmer.

Cook for about 20 minutes, then add the apple pieces. Put the lid on again and cook for another 10 minutes, until the apple is tender but not disintegrating. By this time the cabbage should be well-cooked.

Remove the lid from the pan and, if much liquid remains, turn up the heat and cook briskly until there are just a few tablespoons of concentrated, syrupy sauce left in the bottom of the pan.

SERVES 6 AS AN ACCOMPANIMENT

VARIATION

Add pre-cooked chestnuts (canned or vacuum-packed are fine) towards the end of the cooking time to make the dish more substantial.

# ROASTED MUSHROOMS AND SHALLOTS WITH MUSTARD AND RED WINE

This is a good dish to serve with a nut roast, although I have been known to pile it on top of mashed potatoes and serve it for dinner.

15 g (½ oz) butter (vegans substitute extra olive oil)
1 tablespoon olive oil
230 g (8 oz) small shallots, peeled and left whole
230 g (8 oz) button mushrooms, cleaned and left whole
1 rounded tablespoon grainy mustard, such as *Moutarde de Meaux*
1 tablespoon shoyu or other natural soy sauce
1 teaspoon sugar
230 ml (8 fl oz) red wine

Pre-heat the oven to 180°C (350°F, gas 4) – adjust for fan ovens.

Put the butter in your roasting tin and place it in the oven for a few minutes to melt. Add the olive oil and all the other ingredients. Mix thoroughly, then roast, uncovered, for 45 minutes, stirring occasionally.

SERVES 4 AS A SIDE DISH

# SWEDE AND PARSNIP MASH WITH FRESH HERBS

Many people loathe swedes, but not me. As a child I was fed them mashed with carrots and seasoned with nutmeg and butter, as an accompaniment to Sunday roasts. I much preferred them to the roast beef! Select smaller roots, which are less likely to be bitter or woody, and make sure they are well-cooked. They need to be soft, with no hint of crunch remaining. Like the parsnip that partners them here, they are said to improve in flavour after having been subjected to frost while still in the ground, so make this dish after a cold snap.

1 medium sized swede, peeled and diced
1 medium sized parsnip, peeled and diced
4 stalks celery, finely chopped
3 cloves of garlic, peeled and finely chopped
salt and black pepper
170 ml (6 fl oz) water
either 2 tablespoons finely chopped parsley,
   or 2 teaspoons finely chopped rosemary plus 1 teaspoon
   finely chopped lemon thyme
small piece of butter (vegans substitute olive oil)
2 teaspoons Champagne vinegar or a squeeze of lemon juice

Put the swede, parsnip, celery and garlic in a wide, shallow pan to which there is a well-fitting lid. Add 1 teaspoon of salt and the water, and bring the pan to the boil. Cover, reduce the heat to a simmer, and cook, stirring occasionally, for about 25 minutes until the vegetables are very tender. Add the herbs about 2 minutes before the end of the cooking time. Remove the lid, and if any water remains, raise the heat for a few moments until the liquid has all but vanished.

Mash the vegetables with a little butter and the Champagne vinegar, using a potato masher. Don't use a food processor, as this will make the purée too glutinous. The texture will not be entirely smooth, which is perfectly OK – flecks of celery should remain visible. Add plenty of coarsely ground black pepper, taste, and adjust the seasoning if necessary.

You can serve the purée exactly as it is, or spread it in a shallow oven-proof dish, fork up the surface slightly and brown under a hot grill or in the oven for a few minutes.

SERVES 4–6

# DESSERTS

*There aren't very many dessert recipes here because, like a lot of people, I don't eat very many or make them very often. There are a few reliable and rather decadent recipes which I trot out for dinner parties, and a few sorbets and ice creams – particular favourites.*

# BANOFFI PIE

Banoffi pie has been around in various incarnations for ages. I've tried many, and I think this is far and away the best – the addition of strong, un-sweetened coffee to the cream topping alleviates any potential cloying effects in the caramel layer. This has the added bonus of making it less appealing to children so there's more for the adults. Both the biscuit crumb base and caramel can be made a day or two in advance, if necessary.

Make the pie in a circular dish or cake tin, about 20 cm (8 inch) in diameter, and at least 5 cm (2 inch) deep. If you want to remove it from the tin before serving (rather a nerve-wracking operation), use a cake tin with a removable base, butter the sides of the tin thoroughly and line the base with baking parchment, stuck in place with butter. I prefer to make the pie in its serving dish.

BISCUIT CRUMB BASE

230 g (8 oz) digestive biscuits
110 g (4 oz) butter, melted

CARAMEL

60 g (2 oz) butter
2 rounded tablespoons soft dark brown sugar
400 g (14 oz) can of sweetened condensed milk

BANANA CREAM LAYER

3 tablespoons very strong cold coffee, preferably espresso
430 ml (15 fl oz) double cream (or whipping cream)
3 large or 4 medium-sized bananas, not too ripe
cocoa (or curls of bitter chocolate) for decoration

THE COFFEE FLAVOURING

Make the smallest, strongest cup of espresso coffee you can manage with the equipment at your disposal. If you don't have an espresso machine, pour 60 ml (2 fl oz) of boiling water onto 2 heaped tablespoons of ground coffee and let it infuse for a few minutes before straining through a filter or fine sieve, then set the coffee aside to cool.

THE BISCUIT CRUMB BASE

Whiz the digestive biscuits to fine crumbs in the food processor, then drizzle the melted butter through the spout, with the machine still switched on. If you don't have a food processor, put the biscuits inside a strong, clean plastic bag, wrap it in a tea towel and bash with a rolling pin or hammer to make the crumbs, then combine them with the melted butter in a bowl.

Press the moist crumbs into the bottom of the cake tin and up the sides a bit, using your fingers. No need to aim for machine-like neatness – a little raggedness around the edges adds to the charm of the finished dish. The base should be quite firm though, so as not to disintegrate when serving. Set the base aside for a while to cool and firm up, preferably in the fridge.

THE CARAMEL

Melt the butter and sugar together in a small, heavy saucepan over a gentle heat, until the sugar is completely dissolved. Stir in the condensed milk, and simmer, stirring constantly and rapidly, for 5 minutes. Pour the hot caramel over the biscuit crumb base and leave it to cool.

THE BANANA CREAM LAYER

Whisk the cream for the topping, gradually incorporating two or three tablespoons of the cold, strong coffee. The cream should be quite stiff – soft peaks that will hold their shape – but don't over-beat or you'll end up with coffee-flavoured butter! It will taste quite bitter at this stage, which is as it should be.

Slice the bananas directly over the pie dish onto the caramel and spread them around so the caramel is covered. Pile on the cream immediately, making sure it covers the banana layer completely. This excludes air, preventing the cut bananas from going brown. Chill the pie for at least 2 hours.

Just before serving, sprinkle the pie with a light dusting of cocoa applied through a sieve (practice first over paper), or top it with chocolate curls.

SERVES 6–8

# CHESTNUT SYLLABUB

Although not always very inspired by chestnuts in savoury mode, I adore their flavour in sweet dishes. There is a particular brand of sweetened chestnut purée made by Clement Faugier and imported from France, Crême de Marrons de l'Ardêche Vanillée, which is heaven in a can. I use it to make this very quick and easy syllabub. The slight sourness of the crème fraîche admirably offsets the sweetness of the chestnut purée.

**500 g (18 oz) can of sweetened chestnut purée**
**200 ml (7 fl oz) crème fraîche**
**4 teaspoons brandy or Cognac**

Whisk the chestnut purée for a few minutes to incorporate some air. Gently fold in the crème fraîche and the brandy and pour the mixture into individual glasses – whisky tumblers are about the right size. Chill for 2 or 3 hours. Just before serving sift a light dusting of cocoa over the syllabubs (practice first over paper) or, if you're feeling extravagant, crumble some *marrons glacès* over each portion.

SERVES 4

# CHOCOLATE TOFU MOUSSE

This is a good vegan dessert and also a useful vehicle for persuading children to eat tofu. If you are making this for a vegan, just check that the brand of chocolate you intend to use doesn't contain any animal or dairy products – most dark chocolates don't, but you need to be certain.

100 g (3½ oz) top quality dark chocolate (around 70% cocoa solids)
300 g (10½ oz) silken tofu (firm)
110 g (4 oz) icing sugar, sieved
2 teaspoons vanilla essence
1 tablespoon brandy (omit for children)

Melt the chocolate in a bowl suspended over barely-simmering water. Drain and blot the tofu with kitchen roll, then place it and the remaining ingredients in a food processor and whiz until smooth. Pour in the melted chocolate with the machine running, to incorporate. Transfer to a serving bowl or individual dishes and chill thoroughly. Serve with fresh strawberries or raspberries.

SERVES 4

SERVING SUGGESTION

For an elegant vegan dessert with no whiff of deprivation, serve with a scoop or two of home-made fruit sorbet, such as *Strawberry sorbet* (page 153) or *Seville orange sorbet* (page 152).

# BAKED RHUBARB AND STEM GINGER PUDDING

This is a lovely way of using the first tender forced rhubarb of the season, usually available from mid-winter onwards. Young rhubarb requires no peeling, but as the season progresses the skin toughens, and stringy bits should be pulled off during preparation.

### RHUBARB LAYER

450 g (1 lb) rhubarb, washed, topped and tailed,
    and cut into 1 cm (½ inch) chunks
2 cm (1 inch) piece of fresh ginger, peeled and finely chopped
5 chunks preserved stem ginger, finely diced
4 tablespoons syrup from the stem ginger jar
3 rounded tablespoons sugar

### GINGER SPONGE LAYER

110 g (4 oz) plain white flour
110 g (4 oz) soft brown sugar
110 g (4 oz) butter, at room temperature
2 eggs
1 level tablespoon ground ginger
1½ level teaspoons baking powder
4 chunks preserved stem ginger, cut into 5mm (¼ inch) chunks

Oven temperature: 180°C (350°F, gas 4) – adjust for fan ovens

### RHUBARB LAYER

Mix together the rhubarb, fresh ginger, stem ginger, ginger syrup and sugar, and place in the bottom of a deep oven-proof baking dish, with a capacity of about 1½ litres (2½ pints).

### GINGER SPONGE LAYER

Place the flour, brown sugar, butter, eggs, ground ginger and baking powder in a food processor, and whiz briefly to combine. If you don't have a food processor, just put the ingredients in a large bowl and beat with a wooden spoon or hand-held electric mixer until smooth.

Stir the stem ginger chunks into the mixture by hand. Spread this mixture evenly over the rhubarb chunks, and bake in the middle of the pre-heated oven for about 1 hour, until the top is firm and golden brown. Have a look at it after about half an hour and, if the top is getting rather brown, just cover it with some foil to prevent burning.

Serve hot, warm or cool, with custard, cream or whatever takes your fancy.

SERVES 4–6

# HAZELNUT MERINGUES

These light-brown nutty meringues make a good accompaniment to ice cream, and are also delicious sandwiched together with whipped cream and fresh raspberries or strawberries. They are more interesting in taste and texture than plain meringues. You can vary the size according to their intended use. Tiny meringues make a nice addition to ice cream sundaes and other summery desserts.

**110 g (4 oz) light muscovado (or soft brown) sugar, sifted**
**60 g (2 oz) blanched, roasted hazelnuts (see page 16 for roasting times)**
**2 egg whites**

Oven temperature: 110°C (225°F, gas ¼) – adjust for fan ovens

If the sugar has any obstinate lumps which refuse to go through the sieve, whiz them in a food processor or grind them with a pestle and mortar.

Chop or process the nuts until they are quite small. If using a food processor, be careful not to grind them to a powder – the idea is to retain some texture.

In a large, dry bowl, whisk the egg whites until they are snowy, stiff and glossy-looking (this takes about 5 minutes on high speed with an electric mixer). Add about half the sugar and whisk again, until incorporated, then, using a metal spoon, gently fold in the remaining sugar and the nuts.

Cover metal baking trays with non-stick baking parchment and place appropriately sized spoonfuls of the meringue mixture on the parchment, well apart. Tablespoons are about right for sandwiching, teaspoons for adding to ice cream sundaes.

Bake in the pre-heated oven for about 3 hours, until they are crisp and dry throughout. Smaller meringues will take less time to cook – tiny ones take about 1 hour.

Cool on a rack, then store in air-tight containers until you need them.

MAKES 10–12 LARGE MERINGUES

# BRANDY MOCHA TRIFLE

This trifle is very quick, easy and elegant and is guaranteed to ring anyone's chocolate chimes. I usually make it in individual portions in six glass tumblers (capacity 250 ml, 9 fl oz). It looks pretty and can be served without disintegration, but it can be made in a large bowl if you prefer. It's rather alcoholic, so you may need to warn drivers (or invite them to stay!).

FOR THE SPONGE LAYER

3 level tablespoons light muscovado or demerara sugar
200 ml (7 fl oz) hot strong black coffee, preferably espresso
5 tablespoons brandy
12 or more Savoiardi biscuits (or trifle sponge fingers)

FOR THE CHOCOLATE LAYER

200 ml (7 fl oz) double cream
300 ml (10½ fl oz) milk
4 level tablespoons cornflour
70 g (2½ oz) caster sugar
1 teaspoon natural vanilla extract
1 egg yolk, lightly beaten
200 g (7 oz) dark chocolate (70% cocoa solids), broken into small pieces
4 tablespoons brandy
120 ml (4 fl oz) whipping cream
125 g (4 oz) assorted chocolate-covered coffee beans to decorate
    (there'll be some left over – what a shame)

THE SPONGE LAYER

Dissolve the brown sugar in the hot coffee, then stir in the brandy.

Put two Savoiardi in the bottom of each glass, broken up to fit, or arrange them in the bottom of your serving dish. If you make one large trifle you will probably need more than twelve.

Share out the brandy-flavoured coffee between the glasses, making sure the Savoiardi are saturated.

Put three or four chocolate-covered coffee beans in each glass on top of the sponge layer, positioned so they're visible through the side of the glass, but make sure you leave enough to decorate the tops (three per portion – one each of white, dark and milk chocolate).

## THE CHOCOLATE LAYER

Mix together the double cream and milk. Put the cornflour into a large heat-proof jug and pour on a little of the cold cream and milk mixture, just enough to mix to a paste. Stir it thoroughly to remove lumps.

Now heat the remaining cream and milk to boiling point and pour onto the cornflour, in increments, stirring as you do so. The mixture will thicken immediately. Pour it back into the pan and simmer, stirring, for at least 5 minutes to cook the cornflour, then stir in the caster sugar and vanilla extract.

Pour a little of the hot sauce onto the beaten egg yolk, stirring as you do so, then pour it back into the pan, still stirring. Keep the heat very gentle so as not to scramble the egg, and cook, stirring, for another couple of minutes.

Now take the pan off the heat and add the chocolate. Stir furiously until the chocolate has melted and the sauce is smooth and glossy, and then add the brandy.

Share out the warm chocolate sauce between the glasses, or pour it over the soaked Savoiardi in the large serving bowl. Clean up the glasses if necessary, with a damp cloth.

Chill thoroughly, and top with a little pile of softly-whipped cream just before serving. Decorate with three chocolate-covered coffee beans per portion, arranged like tiny birds' eggs in a nest on the cream.

SERVES 6

# ICES

With the supermarket freezers brimming over with designer ice cream in great variety, you might be forgiven for wondering if making your own is really worth the bother. When I bought a new freezer last year and had some spare capacity, I made a lot of ices and rapidly decided that it is. Ice creams and sorbets made from ripe fresh fruit have a brightness and immediacy that is always lacking in their commercial counterparts. Even something as simple and basic as a lemon sorbet made from fresh ingredients is startlingly delicious compared to the debased synthetic versions on sale commercially.

Home-made ices don't keep indefinitely and should ideally be eaten within 48 hours of making. Nothing dreadful happens if you leave them in the freezer considerably longer than this – it's just that the flavour starts to lose its edge.

Some ices are faster and easier to make than others. I tend to avoid those ice creams that require protracted cooking and stirring of egg custard, partly because they are time-consuming and rather nerve-wracking to make, partly because I dislike using all those egg yolks – some recipes call for as many as fifteen! I like fruit sorbets and yogurt ices – simple, speedy and intense. Although the recipes given here are quite fast, you do need to be around for about three or four hours to give them the occasional beating if you're making them without the aid of a machine. The total amount of time this takes is small, so there's plenty of opportunity to do other things in between.

## HOW TO MAKE ICES BY HAND

All the following recipes can be made in an ice cream machine if you own one, however you don't need a machine to make good home-made ice creams or sorbets. I have been making ices by hand for years, since I broke my machine through over-use! It helps if you have an electric food mixer or a food processor, although neither is essential – you can get by with just a fork. You will also need a wide shallow plastic or stainless steel dish or tray, preferably with a lid, that will fit in your freezer.

If your freezer has a fast-freeze facility it's a good idea to use it. It usually has to be turned on a few hours in advance, to allow the temperature to fall. The colder temperature means the ice crystals will be smaller so the texture of the ice will be smoother, and the whole process is speeded up.

Make your sorbet or ice cream mixture according to the individual recipe instructions and chill thoroughly before freezing. Pour the mixture into a wide, shallow dish, cover with foil or a lid and put it in the coldest part of the freezer. After 1 to 2 hours, the mixture will have started to freeze around the edge. The speed at which this happens depends on the efficiency of your freezer, the size of dish used, etc., so the timings given are approximate. Check after an hour, as you need to catch the mixture at the right moment when some ice has formed but before it is entirely solid.

Remove the dish from the freezer and beat the contents vigorously to break up the ice crystals. Use a food mixer or processor if you have one, otherwise an egg-beater or a fork. Return the dish to the freezer and repeat the beating twice more at 30 to 60 minute intervals.

To serve the ice immediately, return it to the freezer for about half an hour after its final beating to firm up. Most ices that have been in the freezer for several hours will need to be placed in a fridge for about thirty minutes before serving to soften slightly, although ices containing alcohol or egg white are usually soft enough to serve straight from the freezer.

## VODKA LEMON SORBET

The vodka, besides packing a punch, prevents the sorbet from becoming too rock-hard, enabling it to be served straight from the freezer. Don't be tempted to add any extra, or your sorbet may not set. Scrub and dry the lemons before use, and grate off the rind before extracting the juice.

120 g (4$\frac{1}{4}$) oz sugar
270 ml (9 fl oz) water
180 ml (6$\frac{1}{2}$ fl oz) freshly squeezed lemon juice (about 4 lemons' worth)
the finely grated rind from the lemons
3 tablespoons vodka

Dissolve the sugar in about half the water over a low heat. When no trace of grittiness remains, remove the pan from the heat source, stir in the rest of the water, the lemon juice, lemon rind and the vodka. Allow to cool, then chill thoroughly in the fridge.

Either churn in an ice cream machine following the manufacturer's instructions or freeze by hand, following the instructions given opposite.

SERVES 4–6

# SEVILLE ORANGE SORBET

This sorbet is tart and refreshing. It's a lovely thing to make, particularly on a cold, grey day, as the intense citrus aroma given off by the hot orange juice seems to release all the heat and life of summer into your kitchen.

This recipe contains a raw egg white, which is not strictly necessary, but makes for a smoother texture and keeps the sorbet soft enough to serve straight from the freezer. If preferred it can be left out – the sorbet will then be icier, and will need 20 to 30 minutes softening time in the fridge before serving.

**230 g (8 oz) Seville oranges**
**½ litre (18 fl oz) water**
**200 g (7 oz) sugar**
**juice of half a lemon**
**1 egg white, very lightly beaten (omit for vegans)**

Scrub the oranges thoroughly then coarsely chop them, skin, pith, pips and all. Place them in a food processor and whiz, adding enough of the water to prevent the mixture sticking to the sides of the bowl, until everything is quite thoroughly pulverized. Tip the mixture into a large pan, and simmer, covered, for about 15 minutes. Stir occasionally to prevent sticking. If the mixture is too thick and plops alarmingly, like molten lava, add more of the water as necessary. It doesn't matter if you add all the water – it will just take longer to cool down.

Remove the pan from the heat, add the sugar, and stir until it is dissolved. Stir in any remaining water and the lemon juice, then strain through a nylon sieve into a bowl. Press down on the pulp with a wooden spoon to extract as much of the juice as possible. Allow the mixture to cool then chill thoroughly in the fridge.

Either churn in an ice cream machine following the manufacturer's instructions or freeze by hand, following the instructions given on page 150.

When the sorbet is partially frozen add the egg white, but don't beat excessively after it has been added or you'll end up with orange-flavoured snow.

SERVES 5–6

# STRAWBERRY SORBET

Make this in June, when there is a glut of fragrant, ripe strawberries in the garden or shops. It is also a good way of using frozen berries, but don't keep it for very long once it is made. The flavour starts to deteriorate within a few days.

**680 g (1½ lb) strawberries, fresh or frozen**
**150 g (5 oz) sifted icing sugar**
**½ teaspoon balsamic vinegar**
**1 tablespoon Kirsch or other fruity liqueur (optional)**

For fresh strawberries, rinse them in water, pat them dry with kitchen towels and remove the stalks. If you de-stalk them after washing they won't get soggy. Purée them thoroughly in a food processor or blender. Frozen strawberries should be left to soften slightly at room temperature for about 1 hour before puréeing.

The purée can be sieved (using a nylon sieve) to remove the seeds if desired, although it's not strictly necessary. Pour the purée into a shallow, lidded, freezer-proof bowl. Beat in the sugar, balsamic vinegar and liqueur, combining everything thoroughly. The liqueur, besides contributing to the flavour, prevents the sorbet from setting rock solid and enables you to serve it straight from the freezer.

Either churn the sorbet in an ice cream machine following the manufacturer's instructions or freeze by hand, following the instructions given on page 150.

SERVES 4–6

# STRAWBERRY YOGURT ICE

This yogurt ice tastes disproportionately delicious in relation to the minimal effort it takes to make. Don't be tempted to substitute a low fat yogurt though, as the result is likely to be disappointing. As with the previous recipe, it is best consumed within a day or two of making. If you make it with frozen berries it's virtually instant.

**500 g (1 lb 2 oz) strawberries, fresh or frozen**
**125 g (4 ½ oz) caster sugar**
**juice of half a lemon**
**200 g (7 oz) full fat Greek cow's yogurt**

For fresh strawberries, rinse them in water, pat them dry with kitchen towels and remove the stalks. If you are using frozen strawberries allow them to partially defrost at room temperature for about 1 hour.

Put the strawberries, sugar and lemon juice into a food processor or blender and process until smooth. Add the yogurt and process again, just long enough to blend.

Either churn in an ice cream machine following the manufacturer's instructions or freeze by hand, following the instructions given on page 150.

If the ice cream has been frozen overnight, allow it to soften in the refrigerator for 20–30 minutes before serving.

SERVES 4–6

# BAKING

*Baking is easy, rewarding and gloriously self-indulgent. Since the widespread demise of school cookery lessons it seems to have acquired something of a mystique, but so long as you weigh and measure the ingredients accurately, it really is quite straight-forward. However, ovens vary considerably, so take the time and temperature instructions as a guide only. If you don't feel confident, have a practice run at a time when the result isn't critical.*

# HOW TO TELL WHEN THINGS ARE COOKED

### BREAD

Bread should be slightly browned on top. Turn the loaf out of its baking tin and knock on the bottom with your knuckles, as if knocking on a door. If the loaf is cooked it will sound hollow. Loaves that have been baked in tins may need to be removed from the tins and returned naked to the oven shelf for the last few minutes of cooking time to make sure the base is crisp.

### CAKES

Some cakes and baked sponge puddings are tested using the spring test. When you think the cake is almost done, press the top gently with your finger tip, making a slight indentation. If it slowly springs back into place, it is cooked.

Some cakes are tested using a skewer. The clean skewer is inserted into the centre of the cake and removed. If it comes out clean the cake is done, if gooey, cook it a while longer.

If you use a baking tin of a size different to that recommended in a recipe, the cooking time will be affected – deeper cakes take longer to cook than shallow ones.

### BISCUITS

Colour is the only reliable guide. Most biscuits are soft when they first emerge from the oven and only crisp up as they cool. If they are a nice golden-brown colour, consider them cooked. If they are not crisp enough when cold, it's perfectly OK to return them to the oven for a few minutes additional cooking time.

# COOLING

Most baked items need to be cooled on a wire tray, to allow the air to circulate freely around them. This stops them going soggy. If you don't have a special cooling tray the wire or steel inset from a grill pan may make an adequate substitute.

# OVERNIGHT BREAD – BREAD MACHINE RECIPE

I am generally skeptical about kitchen gadgets. Only rarely do they justify the space they occupy; however, I am utterly devoted to my bread machine. I use it four or five times a week, with consistently excellent results, and would now find it hard to live without.

Bread that is allowed to rise very slowly at a cool temperature, with only a small amount of yeast, develops a better flavour than that which is risen rapidly. I first encountered *Overnight bread* at the excellent Herbert's bakery in Bristol, and often had to queue around the block to get it such was the demand. It was a local legend, and the mythology was entirely justified. This recipe is my attempt to re-create their wonderful loaf. I have only ever made it in a Panasonic machine. Different machines vary in their modes of operation so you may need to modify the method slightly to suit yours.

4 g (⅛) oz fresh yeast (a lump the size of a small seedless grape)
up to 270 ml (9½ fl oz) cold water
420 g (15 oz) white bread flour
a pinch of sugar
1 level teaspoon salt
2 tablespoons olive oil

Start the bread last thing at night, or anything between 8 and 13 hours before you want it to be ready. With such a long rising period, the timing is not critical. I've always risen it overnight, when the ambient temperature falls, and have never had problems with dough overflowing; however, if you want to make it during a very hot day, it might be as well to check occasionally that the dough is not rising too fast.

Dissolve the yeast in about two thirds of the water. Put all the other ingredients in the bread machine, add the yeast liquid, and run the pizza dough (or other kneading) programme for 10 minutes to achieve the initial kneading. Keep an eye on the proceedings and add more of the remaining water as necessary, if the machine seems to be struggling or the mixture looks too dry. The dough should be reasonably firm and not too wet, and the exact amount of water needed will vary according to the flour used.

Now re-programme the machine. Mine has to be turned off at the mains for at least 10 minutes before it will allow me to re-programme. Other machines may have different idiosyncrasies. Set the machine for basic bake mode, loaf size medium, and set the timer so the bread will be ready at a time convenient for you, anything between 8 and 13 hours later. The flavour will ripen over the protracted, cool rising period, before the machine does its thing.

If you want a delay period longer than your machine permits, just leave the machine switched off for a time before re-programming.

MAKES 1 LOAF

# OLIVE AND TOMATO FOCACCIA

I make the dough for this recipe in a bread machine, then bake it in the oven, but it is very simple to make by hand if necessary. If using a machine, add the olives, herbs and chopped sun-dried tomatoes towards the end of the kneading cycle to avoid crushing them.

310 g (11 oz) strong white bread flour or pasta flour
1 level teaspoon sugar
1 level teaspoon salt
$\frac{1}{2}$ level teaspoon fast action dried yeast
1 tablespoon olive oil
200 ml (7 fl oz) tomato juice
10 large Kalamata olives, stoned and sliced
4 sun-dried tomatoes in oil, drained and chopped
1 clove of garlic, peeled and crushed
leaves from 2 sprigs of rosemary, finely chopped
extra olive oil for drizzling
coarse crystal salt to sprinkle on the top

Oven temperature: 190°C (375°F, gas 5) – adjust for fan ovens

Combine the flour, sugar, salt and yeast in a large mixing bowl. Pour in the olive oil and tomato juice and mix with a wooden spoon initially, eventually switching to your hands. Tip the dough out onto a floured surface and knead vigorously for about 15 minutes, or until the dough is smooth and elastic.

If you're unsure about kneading, a detailed description of the process is given on page 116. Knead in a little extra flour if the dough is sticky.

Flatten the dough with the palm of your hand, sprinkle over the olives, sun-dried tomatoes, garlic and rosemary, then roll up like a Swiss-roll. Knead again for a few minutes to make sure the pieces are evenly distributed.

Oil a clean bowl with a little olive oil, put the kneaded dough into it and flip it over so that all its surface is thinly coated with oil.

Cover the bowl with a clean, damp tea-towel (or cling-film) and place it in a warm, draught-free place (such as an airing cupboard) to rise until it has doubled in size. This can take from 30 to 90 minutes, depending on the temperature.

Now turn the dough out directly onto a large, oiled baking sheet and punch it down with your hand to deflate it.

Shape the dough, using your hands, into a flat oval, which should be about 1 cm ($\frac{1}{2}$ inch) thick. Cover with a clean, damp tea-towel and put it back in a warm place until it has doubled in height. This second rising will probably take less time than the first.

Heat the oven to 190°C (375°F, gas 5). If you have a fan oven turn the fan off if possible, to avoid drying the bread, otherwise reduce the temperature slightly, following the manufacturer's instructions.

Now stiffen the fingers of one hand and prod down hard all over the surface of the bread to leave a forest of small indentations. Take your olive oil bottle, put two fingers over the spout so as to almost block it, and drizzle oil thinly and as evenly as possible over the surface of the bread.

Finally sprinkle with a little coarse crystal salt before baking for 20–25 minutes, until the top is golden and crisp.

When it looks about done, you may want to slide the bread off the baking sheet and return it directly to the oven shelf for a few moments, just to make sure the base is crisp.

MAKES 1 LARGE FLATBREAD

# SAFFRON CARDAMOM BREAD WITH DATES AND PECANS

A festive morning bread, golden and fragrant with exotic spices – this is a lovely way to start the day on a holiday weekend. Best eaten warm from the oven with butter, it also toasts well. Like my other bread recipes, this dough is easily made in a bread machine, in which case add the fruit and nuts near the end of the kneading time to avoid crushing them. Although I make the dough in a machine I usually shape it by hand and bake in the oven.

If you want this bread freshly baked for breakfast, the dough can be made the night before, given a long, cool rising overnight, and given its second rising in the morning. Like most breads it freezes quite well.

**generous pinch of saffron threads**
**seeds from 20 cardamom pods, finely ground**
**310 g (11 oz) strong white bread-flour**
**1 level teaspoon salt**
**1 heaped tablespoon sugar**
**½ level teaspoon fast action yeast**
**1 tablespoon light olive or groundnut oil, plus a little extra**
**30 g (1 oz) chopped pecans**
**60 g (2 oz) chopped dates**

SUGAR GLAZE (OPTIONAL)
**1 tablespoon granulated sugar**
**2 tablespoons water**

Oven temperature: 180°C (350°F, gas 4) – adjust for fan ovens

Put the saffron threads and ground cardamom in a measuring jug and pour on 2–3 tablespoons of boiling water. Leave to soak for about 10 minutes, then top up to 200 ml (7 fl oz) with cold water.

Put the flour, salt, sugar, yeast, oil and saffron liquid into a large mixing bowl and mix well, initially with a wooden spoon, subsequently with your hand. Turn out onto a floured surface and knead vigorously for about 15 minutes, until the dough is smooth and elastic. If you don't know how to knead dough a detailed description is given on page 116.

Clean out and oil the mixing bowl and flip the dough back into it, turning it over so that its entire surface is lightly coated with oil. Cover the bowl with a clean, damp tea-towel and leave in a warm, draught-free place (such as an airing cupboard) to rise until approximately doubled in size. How long this takes will depend on the temperature – it may be an hour or more.

Tip the dough out onto a floured surface, flatten it with the palm of your hand and, with a floured rolling-pin, roll it out into a large rectangle about 20 × 30 cm (8 × 12 inches), with one of the short sides facing you.

Distribute the nuts and dates evenly over the dough, then firmly roll it up away from you, Swiss-roll fashion. Brush the edge of the dough with a little cold water and pinch to seal the seam. Place the loaf seam-down on a well-oiled baking sheet. Pinch the ends flat and tuck them underneath, to give a smooth, cushion-shaped loaf.

Cover with a damp tea-towel again and leave to rise in that warm, draught-free place, until doubled in height a second time. The second rising should be slightly quicker than the first.

Bake in the pre-heated oven for 25–35 minutes, until the top is golden and crisp. When it looks almost done, you may want to slide the bread off the baking sheet and place it directly on the oven shelf for 2 or 3 minutes, just to make sure the base is cooked and crisp. The base should be slightly browned and should have a hollow sound when tapped with your knuckles. Cool on a wire tray.

For a glossy finish, brush the loaf with sugar glaze immediately after you take it out of the oven. Make the glaze by heating the sugar and water together in a saucepan until the sugar is completely dissolved. There will be leftover glaze, which can be stored in the fridge for about a month.

MAKES 1 LOAF

# CRISP BUTTER SHORTCRUST PASTRY

This is a fool-proof pastry, easy to make and guaranteed not to go soggy. It can be frozen, either before or after cooking. I've given instructions for making a 25 cm (10 inch) pie shell, but the pastry has many other uses. The *Cheese pastry* variation is used in the recipe for *Tomato tartlets with crisp Parmesan topping* (page 29).

170 g (6 oz) plain white flour
30 g (1 oz) ground rice or rice flour
90 g (3 oz) softened butter
pinch of salt
1 egg, separated
2½ tablespoons cold water

Oven temperature: 200°C (400°F, gas 6) – adjust for fan ovens

Put the flour, rice flour, butter, salt and egg yolk into a food processor and whiz briefly until the mixture resembles bread crumbs. Add the water and whiz again, very briefly. Tip out the pastry onto a sheet of cling-film, squash it together with your hands, wrap in the film and refrigerate for at least half an hour.

Pre-heat the oven if you haven't already done so.

Roll out the pastry with a rolling pin on a lightly floured surface until large enough to fit the tart tin. Roll the pastry onto the rolling pin, lift and unroll it over the tin. If it crumbles just patch it together with your fingers, but try to avoid handling or re-rolling it too much – it makes the pastry hard. Cool hands are also a help in this regard.

Press the pastry down well into the corners and sides of the tin, using your fingers. Neaten the edge with scissors, but leave the pastry about 5 mm (¼ inch) higher than the top of the tin to allow for shrinkage. Prick all over the base with a fork, then brush the pastry with the reserved egg white, lightly beaten. On cooking, this creates a barrier to moisture, so the filling will not make the pastry soggy.

Bake the empty pastry case in the pre-heated oven for 15–20 minutes, then pour in the filling of your choice, reduce the temperature to 180°C (350°F, gas 4) – adjust for fan ovens, and cook for another 30 minutes or so, until the filling is cooked.

ENOUGH TO LINE A 25 CM (10 INCH) TART TIN

VARIATION – CHEESE PASTRY

Add 40 g (1½ oz) finely grated fresh Parmesan cheese and an extra ½ tablespoon of water to the initial mix in the food processor.

# ALMOND APPLE CAKE

The combination of almonds and apples is lovely, and this cake is quite versatile in that it can be served hot, warm or cold, with cream, crème fraîche, Greek yogurt or custard.

110 g (4 oz) butter, at room temperature, plus a little extra for the tin
110 g (4 oz) caster sugar
90 g (3 oz) self-raising flour
110 g (4 oz) ground almonds
1 level teaspoon baking powder
2 eggs
2 teaspoons natural almond essence
2 large or 3 small dessert apples

Heat the oven to 180°C (350°F, gas 4) – adjust for fan ovens.

Butter a round 20 cm (8 inch) cake tin and line the base with baking parchment or grease-proof paper.

If you have a food processor, put everything except the apples into the bowl and whiz until well-mixed. Remove the blade and proceed with the apples as described below.

To make the cake by hand, cream the butter and sugar together, until it is pale and quite light in texture. Sift the flour, almonds and baking powder together in a separate bowl. Beat the eggs and almond essence together, then add them bit by bit to the butter mixture, beating well between additions. If the mixture starts to curdle, beat in a spoonful of the flour mixture. Gently fold in the rest of the flour mixture, using a metal spoon.

Quickly peel, core and coarsely chop the apples and stir into the cake mixture. Spread the mixture in the prepared cake tin and bake in the centre of the oven for 40–65 minutes.

The cake is done when a skewer inserted into the middle comes out clean. Turn out onto a wire cooling tray, after first loosening around the edge of the tin with a knife. Remove the paper from the bottom of the cake while it is still hot and leave to cool.

SERVES 6–8

VARIATION – PEAR AND ALMOND CAKE

Substitute pears for apples, but make sure they're not too ripe as the extra juice could make for sogginess.

VARIATION – APPLE OR PEAR UPSIDE DOWN PUDDING

Arrange a layer of extra fruit decoratively in the bottom of the cake tin. The lining paper is crucial if you do this. After turning out, scatter the surface with toasted flaked almonds and serve hot or warm.

# FRENCH CHOCOLATE CAKE WITH GROUND ALMONDS

This is a really good little cake – not big or flashy, just seriously delicious in an understated kind of way. I found the recipe many years ago in a magazine, sadly with no author accreditation – a shame really, because whoever invented it deserves recognition. The cake is moist and dense but light. I often use it as a birthday cake.

Vanilla sugar (see ingredients) is a useful thing to have in the cupboard. Make it by putting a vanilla pod in a jar of caster sugar and leaving it there. Give the jar a shake occasionally. As you use it, top up the jar with extra caster sugar. The vanilla pod will carry on doing its thing for months, if not years.

### THE CAKE

110 g (4 oz) dark chocolate
110 g (4 oz) unsalted butter, at room temperature
4 eggs, separated
110 g (4 oz) vanilla sugar
60 g (2 oz) ground almonds
1 heaped tablespoon plain flour

### THE COUVERTURE

110 g (4 oz) dark chocolate
5 level teaspoons sugar
2 tablespoons water
30 g (1 oz) unsalted butter

Oven temperature: 180°C (350°F, gas 4) – adjust for fan ovens

### THE CAKE

Butter and line (with baking parchment) a round 20 cm (8 inch) cake tin.

Melt the chocolate by placing it in a bowl over a pan of barely-simmering water, then set it aside to cool slightly. Meanwhile, cream the butter until it is pale and fluffy. Use a food mixer if you have one.

Pre-heat the oven if you haven't done so already. If using a fan oven, switch off the fan mechanism if possible, otherwise reduce the temperature in line with the manufacturer's instructions. I find the fan tends to dry out this particular cake.

Beat the melted chocolate into the butter, then add the egg yolks, one by one, beating constantly. Beat in the vanilla sugar. Switch to a metal tablespoon and gently fold in the flour and ground almonds. Whisk the egg whites until they are stiff and white, then fold them into the cake mixture as gently as possible, so as not to lose too much air from the mix. It helps if you stir in a spoonful of egg white first, to 'slacken' the mix, before trying to fold in the rest.

Pour the cake mixture into the prepared tin and bake in the middle of the oven for about 1 hour, or until a metal skewer inserted in the centre of the cake comes out clean. Start testing after about 45 minutes. Turn the cake out carefully onto a wire rack, peel off the lining paper from its base and leave until it is completely cold. It is likely to sink a little, so don't be alarmed.

THE COUVERTURE

Melt the chocolate, sugar and water, by placing them in a heat-proof bowl suspended over a pan of barely-simmering water.  Beat in the butter – the couverture will be smooth, dark, glossy and quite runny. Transfer the cake to its intended serving plate, then pour over the couverture all at once. Working quickly, tilt the serving plate gently from side to side, so the couverture spreads evenly over the cake and down the sides. Don't be tempted to spread it with a knife, or you'll leave marks. Carefully clean up the edges of the serving plate using a damp cloth, then leave the cake in a cool place to set, for at least 1 hour. You could decorate the top with some dark chocolate curls I suppose, but I think that might be gilding the lily. Six or eight blanched almonds arranged round the perimeter would be acceptable.

Serve with very cold thick cream poured over, and a glass of your favourite dessert wine.

SERVES 6–8

# CHOCOLATE BISCUIT CAKE

This is very quick and easy to make, requires no baking, and is brilliant when you need a quick chocolate fix! It needs refrigeration to make it set, but if you're desperate the process can be hastened in the freezer. I make this with Green and Black's organic dark chocolate, which is quite bitter. If you use a sweeter brand, or one with less than seventy per cent cocoa solids, you may want to reduce the sugar content accordingly.

100 g (3½ oz) butter
100 g (3½ oz) top quality bitter chocolate (70% cocoa solids)
3 level tablespoons caster sugar
110 g (4 oz) digestive biscuits
60 g (2 oz) roasted walnuts, chopped (see page 16 for roasting times)

Place the butter, chocolate and sugar together in a heat-proof bowl, suspended over a pan of barely simmering water. The bottom of the bowl should not touch the water – chocolate can go lumpy if heated too fiercely. Leave it to melt, stirring occasionally, while you deal with the digestive biscuits.

Place them in a clean heavy-gauge plastic bag or tea-towel and bash them with a rolling pin, or some other heavy, blunt instrument. They should be fairly well broken up, but not completely pulverized.

Put the biscuit fragments and walnuts in a mixing bowl, pour on the melted chocolate mixture and stir well to amalgamate.

Press the mixture into an 18 cm (7 inch) circular sandwich cake tin and chill until set.

MAKES 6–8 PORTIONS

# SPELT COOKIES WITH DATES AND PECANS

These biscuits are made with the ancient Roman grain *spelt*, and sweetened with honey. The resulting flavour is unusual and deeply satisfying. Honeys vary enormously in flavour, and I always try to find clover honey for this recipe as the floral aroma makes a noticeable contribution. Served with good ice cream and a glass of pudding wine these cookies make a very acceptable dessert.

60 g (2 oz) clover honey, warmed
230 g (8 oz) spelt flour
1 level teaspoon baking powder
½ level teaspoon salt
110 g (4 oz) chopped pecan nuts
90 g (3 oz) chopped dried dates
120 ml (4 fl oz) light sunflower or peanut oil

Oven temperature: 190°C (375°F, gas 5) – adjust for fan ovens

Stand the unopened jar of honey in a pan of hot water over a gentle heat to warm and soften.

Mix the dry ingredients (flour, baking powder, salt, nuts and dates) thoroughly in a large bowl.

Weigh the honey jar with the lid removed, and measure out the honey directly into the dry ingredients by subtraction. Add the oil, stirring until evenly mixed.

Place teaspoons of the mixture on un-greased baking trays and flatten with the back of a fork. If the mixture crumbles, roll it between the palms of your hands to squash it together.

Bake in the pre-heated oven for 10–12 minutes, until golden brown. Cool on the trays for a couple of minutes, so the cookies firm up slightly, then slide them off the trays with the help of a knife and finish cooling on a wire rack.

MAKES ABOUT 24

# TREACLE FLAPJACK

From concept to mouth in less than an hour, this is as good a remedy for the midnight munchies as any I know – just the thing for a sugary but not too sickly carbohydrate fix, and made from ingredients you are quite likely to have hanging around in the cupboard. As all the mixing is done in one large pan, this is also a minimal washing up recipe.

60 g (2 oz) brown sugar
1 tablespoon black treacle
½ tablespoon golden syrup
110 g (4 oz) butter
230 g (8 oz) rolled oats
½ level teaspoon salt

Heat the oven to 200°C (400°F, gas 6) – adjust for fan ovens.

Put the sugar, treacle, syrup and butter into a large saucepan and heat gently, stirring with a wooden spoon, until all is melted and amalgamated.

Take the pan off the heat, stir in the oats and salt and tip the mixture into an 18 cm (7 inch) cake tin (it doesn't need to be oiled). Press down firmly with the palm of your hand.

Bake for about 15–20 minutes, until a warm brown. Cut into wedges while still warm and allow it to cool in the tin.

# COCONUT CARAMEL BARS

Eat with caution – gruesomely unhealthy but cosmically delicious – the choice is yours. Thanks to Laura for this one – a good decadent American recipe and a reminder of our student days!

110 g (4 oz) melted butter
230 g (8 oz) finely crushed digestive biscuits
110 g (4 oz) dessicated coconut
110 g (4 oz) walnut pieces
110 g (4 oz) bitter chocolate (70% cocoa solids), cut into raisin-sized chunks
230 g (8 oz) sweetened condensed milk

Heat the oven to 180°C (350°F, gas 4) – adjust for fan ovens.

This recipe requires a cake tin 16 × 26 cm (6½ × 10 inches), or one of equivalent area.

Stir the melted butter into the crushed digestive biscuits and press the moist crumbs firmly into the bottom of the cake tin and up the sides a bit, using your fingers.

Sprinkle on the coconut, then the walnuts, then the chocolate chunks in layers, and finally pour over the condensed milk as evenly as possible.

Bake for 15–20 minutes and allow to cool for a few minutes before cutting into bars. Don't try to get them out of the tin until they're completely cold.

MAKES 12 BARS

# BREAKFASTS

*Breakfast is probably my favourite meal. It is altogether a more casual and relaxed affair than lunch or dinner, particularly at weekends and holidays. Even if it's just a quick coffee, juice and a slice of toast, I like to savour the moment, preferably outside on my terrace, warming my face in the morning sun and listening to the birds. In winter the prospect of coming home to hot porridge or pancakes after an early morning swim is decidedly cheering.*

*Most of these breakfast recipes are quick, easy to make and soothing to eat – gentle wake-up food – but for those times when only something assertive will do, there are also some zingy, slightly astringent concoctions, using rhubarb, ginger, grapefruit and so on.*

# BREAKFAST PANCAKES – U.S. STYLE

This batter, which makes light, air-filled, American-style breakfast pancakes, can also be used for waffles if you have a waffle iron.

230 g (8 oz) plain flour
30 g (1 oz) soft brown sugar
¼ level teaspoon salt
2 eggs, separated
280 ml (10 fl oz) milk, perhaps a little more
a little butter for frying

Put the flour, sugar and salt in a mixing bowl and swish with a wire balloon whisk, in lieu of sifting. Make a well in the centre and drop in the egg yolks. Using the whisk, start to mix from the centre, gradually incorporating the flour. The batter will get very stiff long before all the flour is mixed in, so add the milk in small increments to make it manageable. Whisk until you have a smooth batter and all the milk has been added, then cover the bowl and put the batter in the fridge for at least 30 minutes to rest. It can stay there for up to 24 hours if necessary.

The batter will probably thicken during the resting period, so you may need to add a little extra milk to regain a manageable consistency. Just before you want to cook, whisk the egg whites (in a clean, dry bowl) until they form stiff peaks, then gently fold them into the batter using a metal spoon.

Heat a little butter for a few minutes in a large, heavy frying pan or griddle, over a moderate heat. Drop a large spoonful of batter onto the surface of the pan. If the temperature is correct the pancake should start to set almost immediately. When you are confident this is the case, drop more spoonfuls of batter into the pan, as many as it can accommodate, but not so many that they run into each other.

When little holes appear on the surface, flip the pancakes over using a spatula and cook for a minute or two on the other side until golden brown, then drain them on absorbent kitchen paper and serve on warm plates with *English apple and blackberry pancake topping* (page 174), hot maple syrup, fried bananas, hot fruit compôte or whatever else takes your fancy.

The pancakes are definitely at their best if served immediately, but can be cooled on a wire rack and re-heated later. To re-heat, put them in a single layer on a metal baking sheet, cover with foil and place in a hot oven for about 3 minutes.

SERVES 3–4

# OATMEAL PANCAKES

These yeasted pancakes make a good breakfast or brunch, with a sweet or savoury topping.

If it's more convenient, the pancakes can be made a day or two in advance, cooled, and stored in an air-tight container, inter-leaved with baking parchment or silicon paper. To re-heat, put them in single layers on metal baking sheets, cover with foil and place in a hot oven for 3–5 minutes.

110 g (4 oz) strong white bread flour
110 g (4 oz) fine oatmeal
1½ level teaspoons sugar
½ level teaspoon salt
½ level teaspoon fast action dried yeast
200 ml (7 fl oz) milk
280 ml (10 fl oz) water
butter or groundnut oil for frying

Put the flour, oatmeal, sugar, salt and yeast into a mixing bowl and stir them together with a fork. Make a well in the centre and pour in a little of the milk. Start mixing in the centre, gradually pulling in the flour from the edges. Add more milk when the mixture feels too stiff to mix easily. Continue gradually adding the milk and mixing, and then do the same with the water. Now cover the bowl with a cloth and put it in a warm, draught-free place to rise for between 1 and 2 hours.

Give the pancake batter a good stir, as it may have separated slightly. If the mixture seems very solid you may need to add a little more milk or water. Flours vary in their capacity to absorb water, so it's impossible to be precise.

Put a very small quantity of butter or oil in a small (15 cm – 6 inch) crêpe pan on a moderate heat. Leave it to heat through for 2–3 minutes then swirl the pan around to make sure it is evenly coated with butter or oil.

The first pancake of the batch is usually rather leaden and you may need to throw it away, so make it smaller than the rest (use 2 tablespoons of batter instead of 3).

Pour the batter quickly into the centre of the pan, then tilt the pan in all directions to make it spread out. Put it back on the heat and just leave it alone for a few minutes, until the surface looks to be drying out and bubbles have appeared all over it. Give the pan a shake – the pancake should be loose; if not, leave it a little longer. Now use a spatula to flip it over, and cook the other side for about 2 minutes. Either serve the pancakes straight from the pan, or cool them on a wire rack for re-heating later.

MAKES SIX 15 CM (6 INCH) PANCAKES

# ENGLISH APPLE AND BLACKBERRY PANCAKE TOPPING

This is one of those incredibly simple dishes that is only as good as the sum of its parts, but when carefully prepared from good ingredients, the dish has complexity and character. If you can find some interesting apple varieties, and you have homemade blackberry jelly to hand, then you have the makings of a minor masterpiece.

The recipe calls for dessert apples, which, being sweeter than cooking apples, need less additional sugar and also hold their shape and texture better when cooked. Use two or three different types of dessert apple if you can; try to include a russet among them. The dish is best made in the autumn or early winter, when the new season's apples are in their prime.

4 medium English dessert apples, mixed varieties
2 tablespoons bramble jelly, preferably home-made (for a recipe see page 209)
sugar if necessary

Peel and core the apples and cut them into chunky wedges. I use one of those gadgets that both cores and slices the apple simultaneously. Unless you are a very fast worker, drop them into cold, acidulated water (water to which a few drops of lemon juice have been added), to prevent them browning.

Heat 2 or 3 tablespoons of water in a large, heavy, frying pan, and add the drained apples. They should fit in one layer. Keep the pan heat moderate and cook the apples gently.

When the apples start to soften slightly dot the jelly around in between them. Shake the pan a little, to mix everything together. The aim is to avoid over-cooking or pulverizing the fruit – it should retain its shape and still have some bite. The blackberry jelly melts and amalgamates with the cooking juices to form a glossy, purple sauce. Taste one of the apple slices and if it seems too tart, add a little extra sugar to the pan.

Serve on hot *Breakfast Pancakes* (page 172), *Oatmeal Pancakes* (page 173) or just on its own, with chilled yogurt or sour cream.

SERVES 3–4

# WALNUT FRENCH TOAST

Crisp and golden on the outside, soft and voluptuous on the inside with the enticing aromas of roasted walnuts and hot maple syrup, this is a truly sybaritic way to start the day.

maple syrup, to serve
butter for frying
3 or 4 thick slices walnut bread, or good white bread
2 eggs, lightly beaten in a wide, shallow dish
a handful of roasted walnut pieces (see page 16 for roasting times)

If you don't have any walnut bread, substitute some decent white bread and use a few extra roasted walnuts.

Set the maple syrup to warm, while you cook the French toast. Either heat it directly in a saucepan, or stand the unopened bottle of maple syrup in a saucepan of hot water over a low heat.

Heat a little butter over a medium heat in a large frying pan. When it starts to foam, quickly dunk a slice of bread in the beaten egg, turn it over and dunk the other side, and put it in the frying pan.  Repeat, with as many slices as your frying pan can comfortably hold. You need to be quite speedy with the dunking, or the first slice will soak up more than its fair share of egg, leaving the rest deprived. Fry the eggy bread until golden brown and crisp on both sides.

Arrange on individual plates or shallow bowls, top with the roasted walnuts and allow people to help themselves to hot maple syrup.  Don't leave the French toast sitting around – it's best served immediately.

SERVES 2

# FRIED BANANA SANDWICH

Does anyone else remember *Cheese Dreams* – a very 1970s dish, comprising cheese sandwiches dipped in beaten egg and shallow-fried? Dated certainly, but no less delicious for that. This is a sweet variation on the theme – less hassle to make than pancakes and, for my money, just as good.

1 banana
1 teaspoon soft brown sugar
pinch of ground cinnamon
a little butter for spreading and frying
2 slices of good bread, preferably walnut bread, but any will do
1 egg, beaten
maple syrup

Mash the banana with the sugar and cinnamon. Butter both slices of bread and sandwich the banana in between. Beat the egg lightly in a shallow bowl, wide enough to accommodate the sandwich, then dip the sandwich in the beaten egg, turning it over so both sides are soaked.

Heat a little butter in a small frying pan, and fry the sandwich over a medium heat for about 5 minutes each side, until golden brown and slightly crisp. Turn the heat down if necessary to prevent burning, but don't reduce the cooking time or the banana won't be hot. Serve with warm maple syrup.

MAKES 1 HEFTY SANDWICH

# FRIED CHOCOLATE SANDWICH

A variation on the preceding recipe, in this chocolate version I don't butter the bread, as the chocolate spread is quite high in fat.

**2 slices of good white bread, such as** *Overnight bread* **(page 157)**
*Chocolate hazelnut spread* **(recipe, page 201)**
**1 egg, beaten**
**a little butter for frying**

Spread a slice of bread thickly with some chocolate hazelnut spread. Put the other slice of bread on top to make a sandwich and press down firmly. Beat the egg lightly in a shallow bowl, wide enough to accommodate the sandwich, then dip the sandwich in the beaten egg, turning it over quickly so both sides are soaked.

Heat a little butter in a small frying pan, and fry the sandwich over a medium heat for about 3 minutes each side, until golden brown and slightly crisp, by which time the chocolate will have melted into the hot bread.

MAKES 1 SANDWICH

VARIATIONS

Instead of chocolate spread, use some really good lemon curd or jam.

# COCONUT GRANOLA

This is a recipe for a crunchy breakfast cereal, variations of which are available ready-made, everywhere. I'm including it mainly for people who might want to make an organic alternative, perhaps to avoid genetically modified soya oil or other ingredients of dubious provenance, but it's also very tasty and a doddle to make.

400 g (14 oz) rolled oats
60 g (2 oz) dessicated coconut
110 g (4 oz) sunflower seeds
110 g (4 oz) sesame seeds
150 g (5 oz) honey
60 ml (2 fl oz) of bland, light oil, such as peanut oil
90 g (3 oz) roasted hazelnuts (see page 16 for roasting times)
90 g (3 oz) raisins

Pre-heat the oven to 160°C (325°F, gas 3) – adjust for fan ovens.

Put the oats, coconut, sunflower and sesame seeds into a large baking tray. Warm the honey and oil together in a small pan over a gentle heat, then pour the liquid into the oat mixture. Stir thoroughly (use your fingers if necessary) to ensure an even distribution throughout the mix.

Bake the mixture for 40–50 minutes stirring every 10 minutes, so that it cooks evenly, until crisp and golden brown. Cool, mix in the hazelnuts and raisins, then store in an air-tight container.

## VARIATIONS

Other nuts and/or fruit can be substituted for the hazels and raisins, to suit individual tastes. Almonds and chopped, dried apricots are a nice combination.

# BREAKFAST BULGAR WITH CARDAMOM AND SULTANAS

This is a slightly exotic version of porridge. I'm not sure where I first got the idea, but it has evolved over time to become a favourite winter breakfast. It requires a little forethought, since the bulgar is best soaked overnight, although if you forget all is not lost – it can be cooked from raw, although it won't be as tender.

PER PERSON
50 g (1¾ oz) bulgar wheat
5 whole cardamon pods
120 ml (4 fl oz) boiling water
small handful of sultanas
a pinch of salt
120 ml (4 fl oz) milk

SERVE WITH AT LEAST ONE OF THE FOLLOWING
hot maple syrup
honey
brown sugar
cream
fried banana slices

The night before you want to eat it, put the bulgar, cardamon and boiling water to soak in a covered saucepan. The next day, add the sultanas, salt and milk to the pan, bring it to the boil, then reduce the heat as low as it will go, cover and cook for 10 minutes. Don't eat the cardamon pods unless you want a major taste sensation!

SERVES 1

# RHUBARB AND STEM GINGER COMPÔTE

This simple compôte is lovely when made in mid-winter with the first, pale pink, forced rhubarb of the season, sometimes sold as Champagne rhubarb. It has a lively flavour, making it good wake-up food, and is excellent served hot with cold, creamy Greek yogurt.

800 g (1lb 12oz) fresh rhubarb
4 pieces preserved stem ginger (in syrup)
110–170 g (4–6 oz) sugar, according to taste
3–4 tablespoons ginger syrup from the jar

Wash the rhubarb, cut it into 2 cm (1 inch) pieces, and place in a wide shallow pan to which there is a well-fitting lid. Only peel it if the stalks are particularly old and coarse. Cut the stem ginger into little cubes, and add it and the remaining ingredients to the pan.

Start with the smaller quantity of sugar – you can always add more later if necessary. Give it a stir, bring it all to the boil and then turn the heat down to the lowest possible setting. Put the lid on and cook, stirring occasionally, until the rhubarb is tender, but not at the point of disintegration. This may take up to an hour, but start checking after 10 minutes – it varies greatly according to the age and thickness of the rhubarb stems.

When the rhubarb is tender, check for sweetness and stir in more sugar if necessary, while the fruit is still hot. If you happen to have the oven on a low heat for something else, the rhubarb can cook quite happily in a covered casserole dish.

SERVES 8

# CITRUS AND PASSION-FRUIT SALAD

In the introduction to this chapter I promised you some zingy wake-up food, so here it is, with a vengeance. I think it's lovely, but fragile night owls might find it a little assertive first thing in the morning. The *pow* factor can be moderated by serving it with some soothing Greek yogurt and maple syrup or honey, or accentuated by a squeeze of fresh lime juice, as you prefer.

Although you can make this in advance, it really is best served at room temperature rather than icy cold from the fridge, so if you have to refrigerate it overnight, try to get it out at least an hour before you want to eat it.

1 pink grapefruit
1 yellow grapefruit
2 blood oranges
2 navel oranges
4 satsumas
3 ripe passion-fruits

The secret of this dish is the meticulous peeling of all the fruit so no trace of pith remains. If you can remove all the pips too, so much the better.

Using the sharpest knife you possess, cut a slice off each end of a grapefruit, to expose two flat circles of flesh. Put the grapefruit flat end down on a chopping board. Use a downward sawing motion and cut off the peel and pith all at once, until you are left with a naked fruit.

Hold the fruit in one hand over your intended serving dish to catch the juice, and carefully cut down each side of all the segments in turn, to detach the fruit from its skin. Collect the segments in the dish, removing pips as you go, and when you've finished, squeeze out the fruit remains (use one hand – keep your knife hand clean) to extract as much juice as possible. Continue with the remaining grapefruit and oranges.

The satsumas are treated a bit differently. Peel them as described for the grapefruit, but instead of trying to split them into individual segments, just slice them across into rings. You can remove the pithy centres if you like. Using your hands, mix the fruit together gently.

Finally, halve the passion-fruits and scoop the contents out with a teaspoon, over the citrus fruits.

SERVES 4 OR MORE

# SAUCES

*A carefully-prepared sauce can really lift a meal, so it's as well to have a few good ones in your culinary repertoire. Although flour-thickened sauces might now be considered a bit old-fashioned, if you get to grips with the basic roux sauce method there are many useful variations.*

*Other sauces, perhaps more modern in tone, are based on a quick whiz of fresh ingredients in a food processor, or the concentration of flavour brought about by reduction.*

*With a few exceptions, I dislike heavy, cream-based sauces, as I find them cloying and prone to congeal. I prefer intensity of flavour to come from the freshness of ingredients such as vegetables, herbs, spices and citrus fruits, and sometimes alcohol.*

# ROUX SAUCE – BASIC METHOD

Here are some detailed instructions for making a sauce thickened with flour, known as a *roux*. It forms the basis for many different recipes, and is an essential part of any cook's repertoire. Once you are familiar with the basic method, endless variations are possible, and some are given in the recipes that follow.

The basics for this type of sauce always comprise:

**butter or oil**
**flour (usually plain white wheat flour)**
**liquid, which can be milk, stock, cream, wine, juice, etc.**

Melt the butter (or heat the oil) in a small but heavy saucepan over a gentle heat, and add the flour, letting it bubble for a few minutes and stirring with a wooden spatula or spoon.

Keeping the saucepan on the heat, incorporate the liquid very gradually, just a few tablespoons at a time, at first. The first addition of liquid will cause the contents of the pan to seize up and set in lumps like instant cement, which can be slightly alarming to the uninitiated. Don't worry, just stir, then beat ferociously, and it will eventually smooth out into a glossy, thick and lump-free paste. Make sure you get the wooden spoon right into the corners of the pan, where lumps may lurk.

The secret of making a perfectly smooth roux is *never* to add the next portion of liquid until you have completely eradicated any lumps that have formed in the pan (otherwise you'll never get rid of the lumps). This involves quite a bit of hard beating.

When the lumps are completely gone, add a little more liquid and repeat the stirring and beating. This will get easier as the mixture is thinned by successive additions of liquid – also, with each addition you can add slightly more liquid at a time.

At a certain point in the proceedings, when the sauce is thin enough, I switch from a wooden spoon to a wire balloon whisk (which is more efficient at dispersing lumps), but this is by no means essential.

When all the liquid has been added it is necessary to cook the sauce for several minutes, otherwise it will taste of raw flour. This can be done either by simmering it gently in the pan, stirring frequently, or later in the proceedings if the sauce is to form the basis of another dish that requires subsequent cooking, such as a soufflé.

# CHEESE SAUCE

Useful for topping a gratin or lasage, as the base for a soufflé or a simple accompaniment for steamed vegetables, cheese sauce is very versatile. This version is more lively than some, with its additions of mustard and lemon juice.

30 g (1 oz) butter
2 level tablespoons plain white flour
280 ml (10 fl oz) milk
170 g (6 oz) mature farmhouse Cheddar, grated
1 level teaspoon Dijon mustard
squeeze of lemon juice (about 1 teaspoonful)
salt and freshly ground black pepper

Make a roux sauce using the butter, flour and milk. Follow the detailed instructions on the previous page if you are unfamiliar with the method. After all the milk has been added and the sauce has thickened, simmer for at least 5 minutes, stirring frequently, then take the sauce off the heat and stir in the cheese. Keep stirring until the cheese has melted and the sauce is smooth. Stir in the remaining ingredients and adjust the seasoning to your liking.

MAKES ABOUT 300 ML (10 FL OZ)

# ONION SAUCE WITH MARSALA

This sauce makes a fine accompaniment to *Terrine of cashews, almonds and apples* (page 90). It's also very good with roasted root vegetables, Yorkshire puddings, mashed or roast potatoes, and so on.

30 g (1 oz) butter (vegans substitute extra oil)
1 tablespoon olive oil
3 onions, peeled and chopped
3 cloves of garlic, peeled and chopped
1 rounded tablespoon flour
300 ml (10 fl oz) sweet Marsala wine
300 ml (10 fl oz) well-flavoured vegetable stock (see recipe on page 208)
natural soy sauce
salt and freshly ground black pepper

Heat the butter and oil together in a large, heavy frying pan and fry the onions over a moderate heat, stirring frequently until they are softened and browned – about 15–20 minutes. Add the garlic and fry for a couple more minutes.

Stir in the flour and cook for a moment or two, then gradually stir in the Marsala and simmer for 15–20 minutes until the liquid is greatly reduced – by about two thirds.

Gradually stir in the vegetable stock, bring the sauce back up to the boil, then season to taste with soy sauce and freshly ground black pepper. Add salt at the very end, if necessary. The sauce can be thinned with extra stock if need be.

MAKES ABOUT 400 ML (14 FL OZ)

# MUSHROOM AND HERB SAUCE

This straightforward sauce is nice with pasta, gnocchi or baked potatoes.

230–350 g (8–12 oz) mushrooms, sliced
15 g (½ oz) butter
1 level teaspoon salt
1 clove of garlic, crushed
170 ml (6 fl oz) dry white wine
1 level tablespoon flour
280 ml (10 fl oz) milk
2 tablespoons fresh, chopped parsley or basil
2–3 tablespoons of cream (optional)
freshly ground black pepper

Fry the mushrooms in the butter, in a shallow frying pan over a medium heat, stirring occasionally. After a moment or two, add the salt and, when the mushrooms start to change colour, add the garlic and start adding the wine. Add a little at a time, and allow it to reduce before adding the next portion – this stops the mushrooms from going soggy and concentrates the wine flavour. Turn the heat up high and allow the wine to sizzle and reduce until it has virtually all evaporated. Stir occasionally to make sure the mushrooms don't stick.

Now turn the heat down and stir in the flour, using a wooden spoon. Start to add the milk gradually, stirring well and eliminating all lumps after each addition. Simmer the sauce over a very gentle heat for about 15 minutes, stirring occasionally. Just before serving stir in the chopped herbs, cream if you're using it, and adjust the seasoning.

MAKES ABOUT 300 ML (10 FL OZ)

# GARLIC MUSHROOM SAUCE

This is another nice, straightforward sauce for pasta, gnocchi, baked potatoes, etc.

230 g (8 oz) mushrooms, thickly sliced
15 g (½ oz) butter
1 tablespoon olive oil
salt and freshly ground black pepper
100 ml (3½ fl oz) single cream
100 g (3½ oz) cream cheese with garlic and herbs
   (soft goat's cheese can also be used)
about 1 tablespoon fresh lemon juice

Fast-fry the mushrooms in the butter and olive oil over quite a high heat. Add 1 teaspoon salt at this stage. Keep stirring to prevent them from sticking, and continue to cook them until they are quite well browned. Add the cream, stir and lower the heat. Cook for about 2 minutes, to reduce slightly. Just before serving stir in the cream cheese just until it has melted. Brighten with the lemon juice and add a generous grinding of black pepper.

SERVES 2–3 ON PASTA

# ORIENTAL PEANUT AND SESAME SAUCE

Although this sauce uses several ingredients, it is very quick and easy to make, and requires no cooking. Most of the ingredients are things that you may already have in the pantry. The sauce will keep for several days in the fridge (minus the spring onions), and is good with Chinese food, or simple steamed or stir-fried vegetables. It can be heated in a pan or microwave, or served at room temperature.

2 level teaspoons sugar
1 tablespoon sesame oil
1 tablespoon dark Chinese vinegar
2 tablespoons tahini
2 tablespoons peanut butter
2 tablespoons soy sauce
1 fresh red chilli, finely chopped
2–3 teaspoons finely chopped fresh ginger
boiling water
a couple of finely sliced spring onions

In a measuring jug, mix together everything except the spring onions and water, using a fork, then gradually stir in some boiling water, until you have 230 ml (8 fl oz) of sauce in total. The amount of water can be varied slightly according to the texture required.

If you are serving the sauce hot, add the spring onions after heating and just before serving to retain some crispness of texture.

MAKES ABOUT 230 ML (8 FL OZ)

# SWEET CHILLI DIPPING SAUCE

This smooth dipping sauce, a pukka version of the type sold in bottles in Asian supermarkets, is both fiery and sweet. Exactly how fiery will depend on the type of chillies used. It is perfectly feasible to reduce the quantity of chillies, should you so desire. Bear in mind though that the sauce needs to be quite intense as it is only used in very small amounts.

30 g (1 oz) red chillies, de-seeded and chopped
5 cloves garlic, peeled
1 sweet red pepper, de-seeded, de-veined and coarsely chopped
1 large or 2 small onions, peeled and coarsely chopped
a thumb-sized piece of fresh ginger, peeled and chopped
1 tablespoon groundnut oil
90 g (3 oz) sugar
4 tablespoons rice vinegar
1 level teaspoon cornflour
4 tablespoons cold water
1½ level teaspoons salt
1 teaspoon sesame oil
2 teaspoons fresh lemon juice

Put the chillies, garlic, red pepper, onions and ginger into a food processor and whiz to a smooth paste, scraping the mixture down into the bowl with a spatula if necessary.

Heat the oil in a small saucepan, add the paste and cook gently, stirring occasionally for 10 minutes. Add the sugar and vinegar to the pan, stir until dissolved and continue cooking for a further 10 minutes.

Mix the cornflour with 1 tablespoon of the cold water in a large jug and pour on some of the hot sauce. Stir, and add the remainder of the sauce, mixing it all together thoroughly. Tip the sauce back into the pan, stir in the rest of the cold water and bring the sauce back to simmering point, stirring constantly, until the sauce thickens slightly and goes glossy. Stir in the salt, sesame oil and lemon juice.

Finally, put the sauce through a medium mesh nylon sieve, pressing down on the solids with the back of a spoon to extract as much liquid as possible. If the sauce seems too thick just thin it with a little extra water – it should be the consistency of pouring cream.

The sauce is excellent served at room temperature (not chilled) with hot *Mushroom and aubergine wontons* (page 30). Give people separate small portions in tiny dishes or ramekins for dipping.

It can also be used as a last-minute addition to stir fries. If put in an air-tight container it will keep in the fridge for a few days, so can be prepared in advance.

MAKES JUST OVER 250 ML (9 FL OZ)

# PESTO

Nothing original about pesto I'm afraid, but that doesn't prevent it from being one of the most delicious sauces in existence, for pasta, potatoes, soups, bread, just about anything. It's very easy to make, and since homemade is vastly superior to anything you can buy in a shop, here is my version. If you can grow or otherwise obtain basil in large quantities, it is easy enough to multiply up the amounts given here. Pesto freezes very successfully – use large ice-cube trays or bun (muffin) tins to open-freeze it in manageable portions, then transfer them to polythene freezer bags.

30 g (1 oz) basil leaves, washed and drained
2 cloves of garlic, crushed
40 g (1 ½ oz) fresh Parmesan cheese, grated
70 g (2 ½ oz) pine kernels
3 tablespoons olive oil
¼ level teaspoon salt
2 tablespoons water

Put all the ingredients into a food processor or blender and whiz until smooth. You may need to stop the machine a couple of times and scrape the sauce down onto the blades. You can use extra olive oil and omit the water if you prefer, but I like the slightly less rich version obtained by using part water. Pesto can be stored in a jar in the fridge for a few days, and will stay fresh for longer if you cover the surface with a layer of olive oil.

SERVES 4 GENEROUSLY, ON PASTA

VARIATION – PESTO BUTTER

Omit the water and mix the sauce with 110 g (4 oz) of softened butter. Use to make *Pesto bread* (page 198), etc.

# TOMATO COULIS

This sauce is only worth making with really well-flavoured, ripe tomatoes. It is cooked very briefly, so the fresh tomato taste is retained. If you have to make it with tomatoes that are anything less than perfect, a little sugar may be needed in the final seasoning.

1 tablespoon olive oil
15 g (½ oz) butter (vegans substitute extra oil)
2 large onions, peeled and very finely chopped
    (in a food processor if you have one)
2 cloves of garlic, peeled and finely chopped
4 large, ripe tomatoes, peeled and puréed before cooking
salt and freshly ground black pepper
sugar, if necessary

Warm the oil and butter together in a heavy frying pan. Add the onion and fry over a moderate heat for about 10 minutes, until soft. Add the garlic and fry for 2 minutes more, then add the raw tomato purée. Simmer, with the pan uncovered, for about 3 minutes, then season to taste with salt, pepper and sugar if necessary.

# SUMMER TOMATO SAUCE WITH BASIL AND CREAM

This is a lovely way of using luscious, sun-ripened home-grown tomatoes, either fresh or frozen. I often serve it on plain pasta, either dry or fresh, and pass round a bowl of grated fresh Parmesan cheese at the table. It also goes very well with *Courgette Ribbon Noodles* (page 123), baked potatoes, gnocchi, etc. The tomatoes are cooked very briefly, and so keep much of the freshness of flavour normally associated with their raw state.

Lettuce-leaf basil is a beautiful, large-leaved form of common green basil. I grow it from seed and have never seen it on sale. The flavour is virtually indistinguishable from that of ordinary basil.

2 medium-sized onions, peeled and chopped
1 tablespoon olive oil
15 g (½ oz) butter
salt
3 cloves of garlic, crushed
4 large or 6 medium ripe tomatoes, peeled and coarsely chopped
no more than 60 ml (2 fl oz) double cream
4 large leaves of lettuce-leaf basil
    or about 20 leaves of ordinary green basil, shredded

In a heavy, wide, shallow pan fry the onions in the oil and butter mixture over a moderate heat until well softened. Add a little salt – about a teaspoonful – then the garlic, followed by the tomatoes.

Cook quite briskly until the tomatoes are slightly reduced, stirring frequently. This should take no more than 10 minutes. Taste and add extra salt if needed, then stir in the cream.

Remove from the heat and stir in the shredded basil just before serving.

SERVES 2–3, ON PASTA

# RED ONION AND REDCURRANT RELISH

Serve warm or cold with any kind of nut roast. This relish also makes a good addition to cheese sandwiches.

3 large or 5 small red onions, peeled and sliced into rings
1 tablespoon olive oil
110 ml (4 fl oz) white wine
100 ml (3½ fl oz) white wine vinegar
1 tablespoon balsamic vinegar
110 g (4 oz) dark brown sugar
60 g (2 oz) redcurrants, fresh or frozen

Sauté the onions in the olive oil over a moderate heat, stirring frequently, until softened but not browned. Add the wine and vinegars, and simmer, with the pan uncovered for 40 minutes. Make sure the heat is not so fierce that the pan boils dry. Stir in the sugar and continue cooking for about another 10 minutes until the liquid is reduced to a thick syrup. Turn up the heat if necessary, to boil off excess liquid. Stir in the redcurrants and cook for just 2 minutes more, so they are softened but still intact.

# SNACKS, SANDWICHES AND TREATS

*In the summer months I could dine contentedly on snacks alone for weeks at a time. When salad vegetables and fruit are plentiful, they need little preparation to give of their best, providing fuss-free, fantastic fast food. My snacking has reached new heights since the acquisition of a bread machine – sandwiches these days are consistently sublime. That's the healthy side of it. I can't pretend the chocolate spread is anything other than unalloyed indulgence, but if you're going to indulge, it may as well be with something worth opening your mouth for!*

# HERB PANCAKES

These small, light pancakes make a lovely accompaniment to just about any savoury dish or, spread with butter and perhaps a slice of cheese, make a good breakfast or snack in their own right. They can provide the carbohydrate element in a meal, taking the place of pasta, grain or potatoes. Vary the herb according to what you're serving them with.

110 g (4oz) plain white flour
salt and freshly ground black pepper
1 egg, separated
140 ml (5 fl oz) milk
1 or 2 tablespoons chopped fresh herbs, depending on the strength
    of the herb chosen (see below for suggestions)
15 g (½ oz) butter
1 tablespoon olive oil

Put the flour, salt and pepper into a mixing bowl and mix with a wire balloon whisk to combine them and remove any lumps. Make a well in the centre and drop in the egg yolk. Using the whisk, start to mix from the centre, gradually incorporating the flour.

The batter will get very stiff before all the flour is mixed in, so start adding the milk in small quantities, to make it manageable. Whisk until all the milk has been added and you have a smooth batter with no lumps, then cover the bowl and put the batter in the fridge for at least 30 minutes to rest. It can stay there for up to 24 hours if necessary.

The batter will probably thicken during the resting period, and you may need to add a little extra milk to regain a manageable consistency. Just before you want to cook, stir in the chopped fresh herbs and, in a separate dry bowl, whisk the egg white until it forms stiff peaks, then gently fold it into the batter using a metal spoon.

Heat the butter and olive oil for a few minutes in a large, heavy frying pan. Drop a tablespoon of batter onto the surface of the pan. If the temperature is correct the pancake should start to set almost immediately. When you are confident this is the case, drop more spoonfuls of batter into the pan, as many as it can accommodate, but not so many that they run into each other.

When little holes appear on the surface, flip the pancakes over using a spatula and cook for a minute or two on the other side until golden brown, then drain on absorbent kitchen paper.

The pancakes are really at their best if served immediately, but can be cooled on a wire rack and re-heated later. To re-heat, put them in a single layer on a metal baking sheet, cover with foil and place in a hot oven for about 3 minutes.

SERVES 2

VARIATIONS

- Rosemary pancakes with *Roasted Mediterranean vegetables with herbs and goat's cheese* (page 113).
- Coriander pancakes with *Freash tomato and pepper salsa* (page 28), *Guacamole* (page 54) and sour cream or yogurt.
- Spiced pepper pancakes – cook a finely chopped sweet red pepper with a few ground cumin and coriander seeds in a little olive oil, then add to batter in place of herbs. Serve with *Tomato and pepper ragoût with grilled goat's cheese* (page 125).
- Chilli and coriander pancakes – add half a finely chopped Habanero pepper and some fresh coriander leaves to the pancake batter. Serve with Mexican food.

# PESTO BREAD

This is an easy variation on garlic bread, and is particularly good as an accompaniment for tomato-based dishes, such as *Cream of tomato soup with basil* (page 42).

**200 g (7 oz) pesto sauce, bought or home-made (recipe on page 191)**
**1 large baguette, or other nice bread**
**110 g (4 oz) butter, at room temperature**

Pre-heat the oven to 200°C (400°F, gas 6) – adjust for fan ovens.

Make pesto butter by mixing the pesto and butter together, using a fork. Cut the baguette into angled 2 cm (1 inch) slices, keeping them in order. Sandwich them all back together again with the pesto butter, which should be spread quite thickly. There may be a little pesto butter left over, depending on the size of your loaf. Wrap the loaf in foil and place directly on the oven shelf for 20 minutes. Serve immediately.

SERVES 4


# AVOCADO AND WALNUT TOAST WITH CHERRY TOMATOES

A delicious snack at almost any time of year, this makes a good quick lunch for one.

**2 slices of toast, made with good wholegrain bread**
**mayonnaise**
**slices or chunks of ripe avocado**
**fresh lime juice**
**salt and freshly ground black pepper**
**a few ripe cherry tomatoes, halved**
**a few roasted walnut pieces (see page 16 for roasting times)**
**fresh coriander leaves**

Spread the toast with mayonnaise. Arrange the avocado on it in a thick layer. Sprinkle lightly with lime juice and salt. Tuck some chunky halves of cherry tomato among the avocado and top with a few walnut pieces. Add more salt and pepper to taste. Top with a few fresh coriander leaves.

SERVES 1

# SUMMER SANDWICH WITH WALNUTS, BABY BROAD BEANS AND EMMENTAL CHEESE

This is one of the most delicious sandwiches known to woman, and simplicity itself to make. Although it is nicest when made with tiny young beans fresh from the garden, it is also more than acceptable made with frozen baby broad beans. There has been a fad recently, at least among cookery writers, for removing the skins from broad beans after cooking, but if life is too short to stuff a mushroom, it's certainly too short for fiddling about with broad bean skins, and burning your fingers into the bargain. If you grow your own, they'll be tender anyway, and if not, they'll still taste good and you can feel virtuous for eating the fibre!

Use the best Emmental you can find, preferably cut off a big slab from a reputable cheese merchant. It varies quite a bit, and the pre-packed supermarket chunks can be very insipid. If the roasting of walnuts seems like a lot of trouble for the sake of a sandwich, bear in mind that they can be roasted in bulk, allowed to cool and stored in an air-tight container for several weeks. They are such a useful addition to so many salads, sandwiches and other dishes that I like to keep a supply on hand.

I haven't specified exact quantities, as they can be adjusted according to personal preference. Be generous, but not over-generous – balance is all, but basically just make it the way you want it.

lightly-steamed baby broad beans, dressed in olive oil and lemon juice
salt and freshly ground black pepper
fresh wholewheat bread
mayonnaise
lettuce and other assorted salad leaves
ripe tomatoes, sliced
roasted walnut pieces (see page 16 for roasting times)
Emmental cheese, diced

Cook the beans just before you want the sandwich – they should be added to it while still warm. If the broad beans are small and freshly picked, they will take only about 2 minutes in a steamer to reach a state of sublime tenderness; if they are large or frozen, keep testing – they'll take a bit longer. As soon as they are tender, take them out of the steam and toss them in a little olive oil, followed by some freshly squeezed lemon juice, salt and pepper.

Spread slices of bread with mayonnaise. Add the salad leaves, tomatoes, nuts and cheese in whatever proportions appeal to you, but don't be too heavy-handed with the cheese or nuts – they're included for accent not substance.

Scatter the warm broad beans into the sandwich, season to taste and eat immediately.

# TORTA DI DOLCELATTE, PEAR AND MACADAMIA SANDWICH

*Torta di Dolcelatte* is an Italian cheese composed of thin alternate layers of Gorgonzola and Mascarpone. It is a fantastic cheese for spreading – smooth and voluptuous, always delicious and never acrid, as is sometimes the case with other blue cheeses. Like most blue cheeses it has an affinity with pears and it is so good it deserves the finest of accompaniments, hence my suggestion of *Comice* pears, but any well-flavoured ripe pear will do. The crisp macadamias provide some textural contrast.

**2 large slices fresh whole grain bread, about 1cm (⅜ inch) thick**
**Torta di Dolcelatte cheese**
**a few roasted macadamia nuts (see page 16 for roasting times), coarsely chopped**
**1 ripe pear, preferably *Doyenne du Comice***

Spread each slice of bread with a generous layer of cheese. Sprinkle a few pieces of macadamia over one slice. Peel and core the pear and slice it over the macadamias in generous chunks – there will probably be some left over. Place the other slice of bread and cheese on top.

SERVES 1

# TOMATO OPEN SANDWICH WITH BASIL AND BALSAMIC VINEGAR

Good food doesn't have to be complicated. This very simple sandwich can be quite sublime. I like it with a multi-grain bread, but it's also good with wholewheat. Ideally the tomatoes should be at room temperature, or even slightly warm from the sun, when their flavour will be most intense.

**whole grain seeded bread**
**mayonnaise**
**2 or 3 ripe tomatoes, sliced**
**salt**
**balsamic vinegar**
**fresh basil or mint leaves (optional)**

Spread a thickish slice of bread with mayonnaise. Pile it high with sliced tomato, grind some salt over each layer and add a few light splashes of balsamic vinegar. Top with torn basil leaves, if you have any. Mint leaves could be used instead, for a change. A wonderfully invigorating instant lunch for a warm day, or just a day when you need reminding of summer.

SERVES 1

# CHOCOLATE HAZELNUT SPREAD

This is chocolate spread for grown-ups: rich, dark, intensely chocolatey and not too sickly-sweet. I began working on this recipe when genetically modified soya was first introduced and seemed likely to be turning up in every convenience food imaginable, although of course we the consumers were not permitted to know which ones. Like many other people, I suspect, I responded to this unacceptable state of affairs by boy-cotting all processed foods. Most chocolate bars, and virtually all chocolate spreads seemed to contain soya and suffering from severe chocolate withdrawal, this spread proved to be exactly what I needed. Although consumer pressure has now brought about improvements in labelling and choice, I still make this spread because I prefer it to anything available commercially.

The quality of the ingredients is paramount. I use Green and Black's Organic Dark Chocolate, which contains seventy per cent cocoa solids. It is quite bitter, so if you use a sweeter brand I suggest you reduce the amount of sugar accordingly.

The choice of oil is important, as the flavour should be very mild and unobtrusive. I made it once with unrefined sunflower oil and the result was quite revolting. I avoid cheap generic vegetable oils, since it's impossible to know what they contain. I suspect they're full of GM soya . . . Peanut oil is generally a safe choice in terms of blandness, and a good sniff over the open bottle of an unfamiliar brand should tell you at once if the flavour is going to be too intense. In this instance a refined oil is probably better than anything too wholesome! You could of course use hazelnut oil, if you have any.

100 g (3 ½ oz) blanched, roasted hazelnuts
100 g (3 ½ oz) dark chocolate (around 70% cocoa solids)
60 g (2 oz) icing sugar
50 ml (1¾ fl oz) mild groundnut (peanut) oil

If your roasted hazelnuts are pale, put them on a baking tray in a moderate oven for a while, until they are a nice warm brown colour, being careful not to let them burn. Set the chocolate in a bowl suspended over a pan of barely-simmering water, to melt. The bottom of the bowl should not touch the surface of the water. Grind the nuts to quite a smooth paste in a food processor, then add all the other ingredients to the processor and whiz until thoroughly amalgamated. Pour into a glass jar while still warm. Store at room temperature.

VARIATIONS:

- Chocolate almond spread – use roasted blanched almonds instead of hazelnuts.
- Mexican chocolate spread – use almonds instead of hazels and add 2 level tea-spoons of ground cinnamon.

# WHITE CHOCOLATE CARDAMOM TRUFFLES

I make these truffles with Green and Black's Organic White Chocolate, of which I am a devotee. At the risk of stating the obvious, if you make them with cheaper, nastier chocolate they won't be as nice! Similarly, I bash open recently-acquired cardamom pods (they don't keep forever!), remove the seeds and grind my own immediately prior to use. The end result is well worth the mimimal extra effort involved – most definitely worth opening your mouth for!

300 g (10½ oz) high quality white chocolate
1 level teaspoon finely ground cardamom seeds
2½ tablespoons almond oil

Break 200 g (7 oz) of the chocolate into pieces and melt in a bowl suspended over barely-simmering water. Stir in the freshly ground cardamom and the oil. Leave to chill in the fridge for about 2 hours until firm but not rock solid – the exact time will depend on your fridge, the width of the bowl, etc. Scoop up teaspoons of truffle mixture and roll into balls between the palms of your hands. Put them on a plate, not touching each other, and put them in the fridge again to harden for an hour or thereabouts.

Now break up the remaining chocolate and melt in a bowl suspended over barely-simmering water, as before. Have ready a large flat tray lined with non-stick baking parchment.

Using two forks, dip each truffle in the melted white chocolate and coat it thoroughly. Allow the surplus chocolate to drip off and put the truffles on the baking parchment to set. When you've finished dunking, put the tray in the fridge again for a while to crisp up the coating.

VARIATION
Coat the truffles in good quality dark or milk chocolate instead of white chocolate.

# FREEZER AND PANTRY

*Here is a small selection of condiments, flavoured butters and other things that can be used to enliven basic foods. They make cooking easier and more rewarding, and are very useful to have around for those occasions when time, energy and inspiration are lacking. I have included a good general recipe for vegetable stock, which freezes well and can be modified to suit the dish for which it is intended.*

# SOME USEFUL THINGS TO FREEZE

### FRESH HERBS

I think that green herbs such as lovage, parsley, tarragon and mint are better frozen than dried. Although no good for salads after freezing, their flavour in cooked dishes is much better than that of the dried equivalent. I just wash them and remove the chunkier stalks, then dry them gently on kitchen paper before freezing them in plastic freezer bags. You can chop or crumble them very easily from their frozen state.

### FRESH GALINGAL, LIME LEAVES AND OTHER SPICES

Galingal, ginger, fresh coriander root, lime leaves and other fresh spices will last quite well in the freezer for a limited period. Pack them well, making sure they are sealed individually in freezer bags to avoid any cross-contamination of flavours.

### CHILLIES

With certain ingredients such as fresh chillies it can be more practical to deal with a large batch in one session, when you're not pressed for time. They freeze well and since you'll have done all that fiddly de-seeding, they're a breeze to deal with once frozen.

In order to avoid stinging fingers and other sensitive body parts, it is advisable to wear rubber gloves when preparing them (don't wipe your eye with a gloved hand, as I invariably do). Halve and de-seed the chillies, wash and drain them, then open freeze the halves, before packing them into an appropriate freezer container.

Chillies vary enormously in strength, both according to, and within, the variety. There's no foolproof way to tell, apart from tasting, but I find that the very hot ones often give off fiery vapours which make me cough when I'm cutting them up.

### SEVILLE ORANGES

It is a good idea to freeze certain ingredients that are very seasonal in their availability. The most important one for me has to be the bitter Seville oranges, which have a very short season of around six weeks. They make a fantastic flavouring, far too good to be restricted to marmalade, and can be used in many instances where you might otherwise think of lemons or limes. I would want them in my freezer if only so I could make *Red onions with Seville orange and Marsala* (page 137), a dish I find it difficult to live without for most of the year. To freeze Seville oranges, simply wash and dry them, then pack them into freezer bags. Use a drinking straw to suck as much air as possible out of the bags before freezing.

# HERB BUTTERS

Herb butters are very useful to have in the freezer. They can be spread on bread, used to flavour simply-cooked grains, vegetables or a sandwich, melted over a stack of savoury pancakes – the possibilities are endless. Rolled into logs then sliced, they look very pretty.

110 g (4 oz) butter, at room temperature
salt (unless your butter is quite salty)
one of the following fresh herbs, washed, dried and finely chopped:
 2 tablespoons of tarragon
 2 tablespoons of chervil
 2 tablespoons of basil
 2 tablespoons of chives
 1 tablespoon of rosemary
 1 tablespoon of lovage
 1 tablespoon of thyme or lemon thyme

Mix the herbs into the butter with a fork, and add salt if necessary. Pile the butter onto a rectangle of grease-proof or silicon paper and form it into a rough log shape. Roll the paper around it and twist the ends to shape the butter into a cylinder approximately 2 cm (1 inch) thick (rather in the style of a Christmas cracker). Chill until firm, then wrap in foil or polythene and freeze.

## GARLIC BUTTER WITH PARSLEY

This butter is so useful it may be worth making double quantity. Used mainly for garlic bread, it also makes a good cooking medium for vegetables, couscous or other grains, laced with a little olive oil to prevent it from burning – great if you're in a hurry or can't be bothered to chop garlic.

1 fat or 2 thin cloves of garlic, peeled and crushed
1 tablespoon of parsley, washed, dried and finely chopped
110 g (4 oz) butter, at room temperature
salt (unless your butter is quite salty)

Mix the garlic and parsley into the butter with a fork, and add salt if necessary. Unless using it immediately, shape into a log and freeze as described in the recipe for *Herb butters* on the previous page.

## LEMON PARSLEY BUTTER

Serve this tangy butter with plainly cooked rice, couscous, potatoes or green vegetables.

3 lemons
1 tablespoon of parsley, washed, dried and finely chopped
110 g (4 oz) butter, at room temperature
salt (unless your butter is quite salty)

Scrub the lemons, dry them and grate off the rind using a fine grater. Squeeze the lemons and strain the juice into a small pan. Simmer the juice uncovered, until it is reduced to about a tablespoonful. Mix the lemon rind, concentrated juice and parsley into the butter with a fork, and add salt if necessary.

Unless using the butter immediately, shape it into a log and freeze as described in the recipe for *Herb butters* on page 205.

# THAI GREEN CURRY PASTE

This aromatic green curry paste is enough for more than one meal, and any paste left over may be stored in a glass jar in the fridge for a few days. It will freeze, but loses some of its bright pungency in the process.

The quantity of paste used per curry depends partly on the strength of the chillies, partly on personal preferences. As a rough guide the amount given here is enough to flavour about twelve servings in total. Although fifteen chillies sounds an alarming quantity, the larger conical green chillies recommended for this recipe are nowhere near as hot as some of the smaller ones.

Galingal is a spice often used in Thai food. It is a rhizome, quite similar in appearance to fresh ginger, light brown in colour with stripes. It can often be found with the fresh herbs in supermarkets, either alone or in mixed packs of fresh Thai spices. It should be peeled before use and either finely chopped if it is to be eaten, or sliced into thin rounds if it is to be discarded before serving. Dried galingal is available, but not recommended, as it lacks the character and complexity of fresh. Since it freezes very successfully, there seems little point in using dried.

This paste forms the basis of *Thai green curry* (page 126), and lends itself to improvisation in stir-fries, soups, etc.

1 level teaspoon coriander seeds, roasted
1 level teaspoon cumin seeds, roasted
6 black peppercorns
15 hot green chillies, the larger type, halved, de-seeded and washed
2 stalks of lemon grass, chopped
3 shallots or small onions, coarsely chopped
1 tablespoon peeled, chopped galingal
4 Kaffir lime leaves, chopped
½ teaspoon grated lime rind
1 teaspoon coriander root, chopped (optional)
1 level tablespoon sugar
1 level teaspoon salt
2 tablespoons groundnut (peanut) oil

To roast the coriander and cumin seeds, just put them in a dry saucepan over a moderate heat, shaking the pan from time to time, until they colour slightly and release their aroma.

Grind the peppercorns, cumin and coriander seeds to a fine powder using an electric grinder (I use a coffee grinder, kept solely for spices) or a pestle and mortar.

Put the ground spices and all the other ingredients in the food processor and whiz to a smooth paste. You may need to stop and scrape the sides of the bowl a couple of times. It isn't a waste of time to pre-chop some of the ingredients, as it reduces the likelihood of stringy fibres remaining in the paste.

If you don't have a food processor, the paste can be made using a large pestle and mortar – just pound everything together until smooth.

# VEGETABLE STOCK

This is a useful and well-flavoured general purpose vegetable stock which doesn't taste overwhelmingly of any one ingredient. It takes a little while to prepare, but is definitely superior to any of the instant stock preparations I've tried, and hence worth bothering with for a special meal. It's actually nice enough to use on its own as a vegetable consommé. By all means vary the vegetables to suit your recipe, but don't skimp on quantities or the flavour will suffer.

Many recipes for stock tell you to fry the vegetables in oil or butter before adding water. I don't find this makes any perceptible difference to the end result, so I don't bother.

If, like me, you get irritated by those little bits of whole nutmeg that are left over when you've grated as much as you can without grating your fingers, you may be pleased to find a use for them here.

3 onions, peeled and coarsely chopped
4 stalks of celery, washed and coarsely chopped
3 carrots, washed but not peeled, and coarsely chopped
4 cloves of garlic, peeled and coarsely chopped
1 large potato, washed but not peeled, and chopped
1 bay leaf
$\frac{1}{2}$ teaspoon dried *herbes de Provence*
8 whole peppercorns: black, white or green
2 nutmeg ends, or a generous grating of nutmeg
170 ml (6 fl oz) dry white wine
1 litre (35 fl oz) water

Put all the ingredients in a large pan and bring up to the boil. Cover and simmer gently for 40 minutes. Strain the stock through a fine sieve, discarding the vegetables.

The strained stock can be cooked in an open pan to reduce it and further intensify the flavour, if necessary. I do this if I want to freeze the stock, as it then occupies less space. It can, of course, be diluted again subsequently. Unless you are using it immediately, cool the stock rapidly by standing the open pan in a sink of cold water, and refrigerate or freeze.

MAKES JUST UNDER 1 LITRE (1$\frac{3}{4}$ PINTS)


VARIATIONS

Some (but not all) of the following could be added to the basic recipe: pumpkin or squash (de-seeded and scrubbed but not peeled), leeks (including the green part), chard stems, celeriac, broccoli trimmings, parsley, tomato skin and seeds.

# BRAMBLE JELLY

This is such a delicious preserve it's worth getting lacerations for, as you surely will if you pick wild blackberries. Although cultivated berries may yield more juice, I'm not convinced their flavour is as good. The quantities given are modest, but if you're made of stern enough stuff and have the tenacity to keep picking, the recipe can be bulked up easily.

The jelly is nice on its own, just with bread or toast, and is an essential ingredient in *English apple and blackberry pancake topping* (page 174). It also makes a good flavouring for sorbets, ice cream or just plain Greek yogurt.

**1 kg (2 lb) wild blackberries**
**juice of 1 lemon**
**230 ml (8 fl oz) water**
**sugar (to calculate the amount see below)**

Wash the fruit thoroughly, then put it in a large, heavy-based pan, preferably stainless steel, with the lemon juice and water. Bring it to the boil, then cover and simmer gently until the fruit is tender (about 30 minutes). Mash (or briefly food process) the cooked berries, then strain and collect the juice through a jelly bag (or sieve lined with muslin) allowing it to finish dripping naturally. Don't squeeze the muslin or the jelly will be cloudy.

After straining, measure the juice and calculate the sugar, allowing 60 g sugar per 100 ml juice (12 oz sugar per 20 fl oz juice). Return the juice to a clean pan, bring it to the boil then add the sugar, stirring until it is dissolved. Boil rapidly until setting point is reached (about 10 minutes).

To test for a good set, have ready a small plate chilling in the freezer. Spoon a teaspoon or less of jelly onto the cold plate, and tilt the plate so it spreads as much as possible. Leave to cool for about 30–40 seconds, then push your finger across the surface of the jelly. If it wrinkles then it's ready. If it's still completely liquid with no trace of wrinkling, cook it for a few minutes longer and try again.

Skim off any froth using a slotted spoon, then pour into pre-warmed sterilized jars (see below) and seal immediately. If you plan to keep the jelly for any length of time, make sure to fill the jars right to the top – the less air space, the less likelihood of bacteria or moulds breeding. For the same reason, it's a good idea to put the lids on while the jelly is still very hot.

TO STERILIZE JARS

Put clean, dry jars in a moderate oven for at least 10 minutes. I generally sterilize the lids using babies' bottle-sterilizing liquid.

# INDEX